THE PRACTICAL GUIDE FOR CREATIVE ENTREPRENEURS,
COACHES, AND SMALL BUSINESSES TO BUILD YOUR BRAND AND
GROW YOUR BUSINESS ONLINE

We Mean BUSINESS

CHRISTINE HANSEN

Publishing Services provided by Paper Raven Books

Printed in the United States of America

First Printing, 2021

Paperback ISBN= 979-8-9857606-0-6
Hardback ISBN= 979-8-9857606-1-3

TABLE OF CONTENTS

INTRODUCTION

Dear reader (oh my now it's real),

My biggest wish when it came to creating this book was to provide you with all the essentials, plus elements that will make you shine even brighter, to start or grow your online business.

THE book in which you get absolutely everything you need in one volume without making you feel overwhelmed or out of your element. It was really important for me that this is not one of those sales traps we see all the time where the book only scratches the surface, and you have to sign up to get more *(haven't come across one of those yet? Trust me, you will. It's all the rage in the online biz world)*. Now, in all honesty, if you reached out and wanted to work with me to go more in depth after your read then I would not be repulsed to the idea, au contraire, I'd be very happy! But my true wish is that **this** is the ultimate volume that provides you with all the tools, as well as the right mindset, to run your best online business.

Now, this book started as a podcast that I ran with my business bestie, Kendra Perry, for two years. We had such an amazing time, chatting about all the knowledge we learned and developed and interviewing amazing people with a wealth of experience – I just really didn't want all this knowledge, plus everything we have learned during our journeys, to simply go away!

Hence this book is here to serve everyone who has the idea for a business and the wish and passion to make their best business come true (or those who have a business and want to see it thrive even further).

I have really found my place in the crazy world of internet-land business, and I wanted to create a book that is based on my main true values: honesty, authenticity, and kindness. Of course, my book is also practical and will give you all the tools to avoid blind spots and pitfalls.

There is no need to do anything that you don't feel comfortable with on this journey, even if some online business gurus swear that that is the only blueprint to success and their testimonials seem overwhelming. I am here to give you options and am also inviting you throughout to regularly check in with yourself whether you are still true to yourself so that you are growing a business you'll love.

Rather than building a successful business but not being able to enjoy it because you approached creating it the wrong way.

"Lighthouses don't go running all over an island looking for boats to save; they just stand there shining."

Anne Lamott

Be a lighthouse.

My belief is that every one of us who wants to serve people is like a lighthouse. The ocean is full of little boats with people that are ready to be rescued in the area you can serve them or who feel an inkling that there is something for them out there. They see these different lighthouses (sometimes very similar and yet always unique, because, you know, there is only one of **you**), and they will connect with one of them. The one they relate to the most. Hence, there is no need for a sense of competition because we are all different, even if we serve with the same thing.

And **then it's up to them** whether they take action and row to the lighthouse or not. But the lighthouse never moves. It doesn't suddenly hop towards the beach to rescue those boats. Aka you: You shouldn't bend and twist to make people want to work with you either.

That is how I see our businesses: it's never up to us to bend and compromise, to run towards the beach. We're here with our knowledge, with everything we've learned through experience and through the courses we've taken. We are who we are, and by shining that light and by marketing ourselves that way with our own individuality, we will automatically attract the right clients. (*More on that in Section 1.*)

This book is me shining my light. If you've picked it up, it resonated with you in some way, and I really want to welcome you into my world. I want to serve you, not waste your time, and I just really wish you all the best for your business.

How to read this book.

You can either go through it chronologically, chapter by chapter, implementing as you go, or use this book as your Bible, your resource, your guide, and pick out the chapters you want to read. Some chapters are based on interviews with amazing experts *(find all of their details at the end of the book.)* I've also included some cheeky deals you'll get if you tell them you come from me! As well as an amazing deal for my money mindset course which, might I add, is an absolute essential to shine a light on some mindset blind spots. *(Yes, you may immediately skip to the end at this time to cash those things in, the plot will not be ruined seeing as there really isn't one).*

In between chapters you'll find toolboxes, book boxes, and a nerd box or two. These are extra awesome snippets of information to make your business that much more robust.

Blind Spot Alert:

Remember, building a business always takes time and A LOT of energy. Sometimes you might feel like you've already done everything, especially in the beginning, but what you've actually done is **implementing** everything and setting everything into place, whereas the time you've given to be known and seen by potential clients is minimal. I do not promise to make you a millionaire in thirty days. That is not what I'm about. This is for people who are patient and who know that it takes time. The more you do, the more time you invest, the quicker it will happen for you.

In terms of physics: you will gain momentum. But momentum comes in small increments first. So, celebrate each small success and see them grow and get momentum. It-will-happen!

I'd also love for you to reach out to me if you need me. I'm available for questions in my Facebook group if you want to connect: https://www.facebook.com/groups/christinemeansbusiness and follow me on Insta @bychristine_hansen.

Finally, I just want you to have fun with my book. Don't take yourself too seriously, and I am here for you if you need me.

BUSINESS LINGO 101: TERMS YOU NEED TO KNOW

Right, so you're your own boss of your little (or massive) online business empire. You need to know the lingo. I have been in groups of online courses and programmes where I saw people panicking way too often because the learning curve was just too steep.

So in order to avoid that for you and to keep you from being out of your depth, full of doubts, or confused, I have compiled a handy dandy glossary for you so that you quickly understand what "everyone" is talking about so that you can start your journey full of confidence and ease. Clever, eh? So here we go:

Blog post. *(Chapter 3.3)*

These days, everybody has a blog. Posts don't have to be super long, and they don't even have to be just text. You can use audio, visual, snippets, photos. 500 words is a sweet spot for a regular post. If you want to charm Google and create content that will more likely be picked up by the search engine then aim towards 3000 words (those can absolutely be exceptions and not the norm, no worries). Blog posts should be your primary form of content. (*On everything about blogs, go to Chapter 3.3*) When you set them up on your website, you will notice that you have a choice between creating pages and posts. You will create one blog page, and that page will host all of your blog posts. So, they aren't the same.

Clickbait.

Clickbait is online content with the sole purpose to encourage people to click on a hyperlink without providing valuable information. Often, the content provided is misleading or sensational. Examples of clickbait can be headlines, texts, or thumbnail links. Don't do this. It's just not worth it as it will leave people with a negative connotation of you (and it's just slimy and gross).

Conversion.

In internet-land we use this term in the context of converting someone from cold traffic (aka someone who has never heard of you before in their life) into a lead (aka someone who has engaged with you somehow by either liking a post, signing up to your email list, or joining your online group) into a customer. In a nutshell, transforming someone from somebody who doesn't know you to a client. You can track how many people you convert. You always want a high conversion rate, it's a marker for improvement. If you have a low rate, it means something is not working, so you can tinker around and see what could improve it.

Copy.

Copy refers to the output of copywriters in advertising, marketing, and similar. Copywriters write copy or text that encourages consumers to take an action (i.e., buy goods or services) or be persuaded by a brand *(so it has nothing to do with this thing: ©)*. The term can also be used in publishing to refer to text in books and magazines. Examples of copy can be found in ads, email marketing, landing pages, brochures.

CTA.

Call **T**o **A**ction. Make it as enticing as possible to click that button to get to the next step. Use enthusiastic and irresistible language. For example, on Insta: write "send me a DM." It doesn't always need to be a sell. It could be: click the like, drop an emoji, etc.

Entice to interact.

Funnel. *(Chapter 3.2)*

Your funnel is the path you guide your audience down to becoming future clients. You are funnelling people into becoming your clients. This can take the shape of an opt-in form, a tiny offer (check out Allie Bjerk, the queen of Tiny Offers®), an opt-in box, a landing page, a pop-up, line up, band, or ribbon (we shall go into those a bit below, so don't panic if you are wondering what the heck a ribbon is doing on a website and not in your hair).

That's where your funnel starts. **Once people give their email or purchase your small offer that's when they're entering the funnel.** Business owners use these funnels to get people interested and then qualify or disqualify people. Important: You should always know what you want people to do at the end of your funnel before you even set it up. Email marketing software is necessary as it is designed to send emails to a lot of people and to be marketing friendly *(so please don't use your Gmail account for this).*

TOOLBOX

Email software providers (or ESP) I love:

FloDesk

http://www.christinemeansbusiness.com/flodesk

ConvertKit

ActiveCampaign

MailerLite

https://www.christinemeansbusiness.com/Mailerlite

Leads / Cold traffic.

A lead is someone who is a little bit interested. A prospect.

Opt-in / lead magnet / freebie / free gift. *(See Chapter 3.2 for more.)*

Your opt-in, also called lead magnet, freebie, or free gift is exactly that: a little something you gift your audience in exchange for their email address. It can be a PDF, a list, whatever you want. *(There are best practices in section 3 of the book).*

You should create a separate page for your opt-in. This landing page has one sole purpose and that is to get people to type in their name and email. (In contrast, a website has a menu and options whereas a landing page doesn't so that the visitor has only 1 thing to do: click a button). You can use your website to create a landing page, your Email marketing software, or you can use a separate funnel software. Your landing page can also be called a squeeze page or a lead page. The reason you might want to use specific landing page software in the future is because you can have more complex funnels that way, i.e., multiple opt-ins etc.

Nurture sequence, automation flow, workflow. *(See Chapter 3.2.)*

These are a series of emails sent to prospective clients, in which you introduce yourself, and through different emails, get people to do what you want, which can be reaching out to you or purchasing something for example.

SEO or Search Engine Optimization. *(Chapter 3.1)*

SEO simply means that you do certain things to optimize your content online that helps you be found. For example: use tags, files, alt texts, words, headings.

TOOLBOX

Yoast.

SEO plugin for Wordpress.

Tripwire.

A tripwire is a low-priced product that is offered to someone after they opt-in to get something for free. A new movement is actually to completely ditch the free stuff and only lead with a tripwire or tiny offer. The price tag is usually around the $27 mark or similar to what a lunch would cost you. Hence, not a lot of thought is required, and it is great for impulse buying. If you do keep a free opt-in though, then the process would be to have your landing page to enter their email for their free gift and then redirect to a mini sales page after they entered their details. Offer whatever you're selling at a severely discounted rate, something that is comparable to the freebie. If you're running ads to the opt-in, the tripwire is to recoup some of the money spent on the ad.

You can also use a tripwire in your email sequence because people are more likely to say yes again if they have done so once already.

Website. *(Check out Chapter 2.3 for more on building your website.)*

Building a website is like building a town – your web address is your domain. You need a site where you can build. Your plot = hosting. The host allows you to build your house at that address.

Examples of hosts: Siteground (my fave), Hostgator, or Easy Dns.

Your domain and host are separate and don't need to be from the same company.

A good hosting platform is Siteground because they have a really great support chat. They can literally set up your website for you. Just ask loads of questions. I swear by their customer service.

My fave builders to use with Wordpress (which make designing your website a lot easier) are ThriveThemes or Elementor.

Remember: Wordpress.com (blog) and Wordpress.org (building tool) are not the same!

You can also opt for all-in-one solutions like Squarespace or Wix. However, I found that they can become limiting when you are growing, so they are not my preferred choice personally. But if you are overwhelmed with tech then they are a great beginner's option to get moving versus staying paralysed from overwhelm.

1. Branding

Section 1

BRANDING

Let me be blunt. As I have grown and developed my businesses my point of view on branding has changed many times. I started with the classic client avatar that most people get taught now (i.e., gender, age, hobbies, location, etc.), and I've worked my way towards a value-based brand. That means, I don't care who my clients are (within reason). For me, it's about connecting with your soul clients; those clients who, no matter who they are, click with you on a deeper level. Who share your core values.

My top tip to get your branding right: figure out what your values are and focus on those *(find amazing tips to journal throughout this book!)*. Make it clear who you are and your soulmate clients will find you. Branding is about being yourself and not talking to an audience and hoping they will like you. It is about what **you** like, not what you *assume* they like.

For me, for you, for us.

This section is going to give you different insights, and you can pick and choose what suits your business best.

Remember that lighthouse metaphor from the intro?

Your brand is you.

Your Brand

I have had a lot of different coaches, taken a lot of different courses, and the way I've approached branding has changed a lot over the years. In the beginning, my first coach (and many after that) gave me the exercise to create a client avatar. That is basically creating a profile of your ideal client. You create a sketch of who you think your perfect client is: male, female? What is their age? How much do they earn? What kind of things do they buy? Based on these kinds of questions, you then create a language that you think will appeal to this ideal client. Now, what I've learned is that it's none of our business to assume anything. People are just so different even if they have things in common. My favourite example for this is the niche "mothers." Literally, the only thing we have in common is that we became pregnant, and we gave birth (most of the time, I am adopted, yet my mother is clearly still a mother). But in general, that's it. Everything else is individual: the way we love our children, raise them, our own relationship with motherhood. It doesn't mean every mother is overwhelmed or super busy or carries tonnes of mom guilt or whatever you think you know.

Don't assume anything about your clients.

So again: it's none of our business to assume anything. Instead, I've developed a technique to turn the whole thing around. Remember the lighthouse metaphor from the introduction?

I have made the best experiences with the best clients by only focusing on my own values and the things I like. Because here's the thing: people who like what I like will automatically get along with me! Even if they're very different from me – our core values are the same.

The stuff I like? I love being lazy, I love being efficient rather than working nonstop, travelling, beautiful things in life, luxury, philanthropy for animals, and laughing! And those people who get that, those are my soul clients. We inspire each other. It's an amazing thing. And this is what I want for your business. Attract your soul clients rather than building something on an assumption and then finding out that those people are not the ones you want to work with!

So many people are afraid to narrow down their niche because they think no one can relate to them. But let me tell you, that's just not true. When I set up my business, Sleep Like A Boss, I had super feminine branding going on, but fifty percent of the clients I attracted were men.

Branding helps you to know your niche, which means you don't need to create content for everyone, you can just focus on your essentials and get the job done with ease and joy. So even if you say you just work with women, there might be some men who really crave a more feminine touch, and that will attract them to you. All of us need the feminine and the masculine, so don't worry about that. You will always attract those who need exactly what you can offer the way you offer it.

I like to give the example of MLM companies like Tupperware or essential oils or whatever. Everyone has the same products, training, and tools, and yet you will always be drawn to one particular person. So ponder that idea and hopefully it will help you to realise that there is never competition. Because you are amazing *(or you wouldn't be reading this book because I only attract amazing people, see?)*.

It's important to remember: You will change. That is just how it is. One of your main jobs in running a business is figuring out who you are and that is going to change ALL THE TIME.

Top tip: Don't invest too much in your first website. You will want to change it in six months anyway!

Why Branding Is More About YOU and Less About a Logo

Back in the olden days, branding used to be all about the graphic, the logo, the colours. These days, for service providers (that's you, creatives!) the most important aspect about your brand is yourself. Yep, amazing you. Now, if you're selling a product, it's a bit different. (Still, stay tuned for the rest of the amazing content to come.) But a lot of us are in the service industry, providing our valuable time and expertise to others. The most important thing to remember?

You need to be you.

I know what you're thinking: '*obviously,*' right? But guess what? You being you requires work. It requires personal development. And that can be surprisingly tough.

But don't you worry, I'll show you exactly how to be the best YOU for your business.

"A brand is what people say about you when you're not in the room." (Jeff Bezos)

People want to connect with you, and in order to do that they need to know who you are. So, my advice: Don't spend all your budget on a branding expert in the beginning. Keep it clean and simple. Because you know what? Things will change. I'm now on website number 4. You might change your niche. **You** might change. (Actually, scratch that, you will most definitely change.)

Top tips to finding out who you are.

- Sit down and journal. Whatever makes you feel uncomfortable (comments, situations, behaviours), you need to investigate that.
- What are your unique strengths?
- What are five words that describe yourself?
- What are your core values? What do you stand for?
- Ask family and friends if you're stuck.
- Don't look at what other people are doing in your industry. Don't try and copy. You need to be you; you need to find your voice.
- Struggling with doubts and shame? (We all do.) Get a coach or therapist to help! (Again, we all do!)

Now, all of this doesn't mean you have to be only one thing. I have different personas: I love to get glammed up, I love to be sexy, but I also love to wear sneakers and a t-shirt. Sometimes, as an example: I make a point of wearing relaxed clothes to events where everybody else will be wearing suits – just to say: I can do whatever I want. BUT I've figured out that a good touch of glam is good for my website – after all, I'm all about those high-end clients, plus I really enjoy my designer wear. However, on my video and Insta stories, I'm more down to earth. Sometimes (especially in the morning) I don't wear make-up, and I even talk about being lazy (@bychristine_hansen). It's all part of me just as much as my more polished and ambitious side. Don't force yourself to be something you're not, PEOPLE WILL KNOW.

Here's the thing: If you're authentic, if you're you, you will automatically connect with the right clients.

Top tip: A quick way to finding the right tone for your business is to communicate the way you like to be communicated with and how you like to feel when you get in touch with someone new. Don't fall into the trap of imagining hypothetical dream clients.

Remember: Becoming more confident should not be your ego taking over. And you need to really be honest with yourself. Finding out who you truly are is not always easy. But it makes you real, right? Flaws and all. That's what people connect with.

Don't be perfect. Don't be awful. Be real.

Being you on Instagram.

- Think about what kind of accounts you would be interested to follow – not those with a logo as a profile picture, right? Use a picture of yourself and not your logo (unless you're selling a product). You need that human connection.

- Your name should be in the bio. How else do people know who you are?
- Have photos of yourself in your feed so people can get to know you. You need to make it clear who you are. When I travel, I go to Airbnb Experiences and book a photoshoot. It costs me around $100 - $200 for 20-30 pictures in general. That way, I get great pictures perfect for my Insta feed and blog.
- You don't need a professional angle. If you have a friend who takes good pictures, just ask them to take a picture of you whenever you're out. Be confident, say it's for your job. (You're a star! Well, almost.)
- Portrait mode is great. Use a tripod if you can.
- Have some kind of structure on your feed. If you just want to throw something out there, use Insta stories. I use stories for my more casual stuff. How much I love naps, for example. And I do, I adore naps.

Being you on Video.

Video is such an important tool for your personal branding. It's actually the best way to show who you are. People just connect well with video. It's a fact. (Check out mine: https://www.youtube.com/c/ByChristineHansen/videos .)

Top tip: When you're filming, tell yourself not to expect people to watch. Try not to have that at the back of your mind. Just assume nobody's ever going to watch it. That'll take away so much pressure!

Video is definitely something you need to learn. You'll never be good at it unless you practise. And yes, your first videos won't be great at first; nobody's are and that is okay. It's actually likeable!

Insider tip: Spontaneous videos are often those that get the most reaction.

And once you've recorded a video, repurpose it. For YouTube, your blog, Insta…

Biggest compliment: I feel like I already know you.

TOOLBOX

People to check out and be inspired by:
Laura Belgray https://talkingshrimp.com
Heather Jones https://heather-jones.com
Amber Dugger http://amberdugger.com
Rebecca Ives @beckyivesofficial
Susannah Conway https://www.susannahconway.com/

Now, you know how I said not to waste money on a branding coach right in the beginning? Okay, here's the thing: You cannot do it alone. That doesn't mean getting a branding coach, but it does mean working on your personal development. Whether you start by asking friends for help (see the **tip box** on finding out who you are), or you invest in a personal development coach, mindfulness courses, etc. Personally, I would have saved so much money if I'd started earlier with personal development.

Don't invest in your brand, invest in yourself, and your brand will grow with you.

What if you do want to work with a branding coach? Here's my hot take: they need to understand what you do. As soon as a consultant tries to fit you into a box, run for the hills! They need to listen and design around YOU. See? This is why finding out who you are is so important.

Journaling prompt:

Make a list of your core values,
as well as your dealbreakers.
Your clients need to reach a certain bar to qualify
to work with you. What are your dealbreakers and
requirements for your perfect client?

Influence Your Brand through Storytelling

My story.

I grew up in a pretty traditional setting in Luxembourg. It was very focused on conventional values, academic achievements, getting out into the world, and getting a safe, well-paid job. And that is what I did for a long time. I realised I was a rebel at university but, through one way or another, I continued down the traditional route, and I lived a happy but half-asleep life for ten years. I got married, started a family… Nothing was bad but it was also not fulfilling for me. After I had my little one, I decided not to go back to work and instead started my own business. But my first business was not what I really wanted to do – Sleep Like A Baby was a baby sleep consulting business. Turns out, I don't really like babies (apart from my own)! So, after one year I changed it to Sleep Like A Boss because I loved the sleep market and decided to cater for adults this time around. Changing businesses after a year was quite difficult because everybody tells you not to do it: "finish what you started," it appears flaky, quitting is for losers, etc. But here's the thing: That's rubbish. Those ideas are built on patriarchal, macho-values. You can totally do it. You can do whatever you want! Now, don't pivot at every little problem, but if you know it's really not what you want, then go ahead and change.

So, I had my Sleep Like A Boss business and what I discovered then was that I loved building up the business more than I did working with my clients (even though I had amazing clients). What I did was I built a team to hand my clients over to and I focused on running the business. Then I decided that I wanted to start helping other people build their businesses online too. And that is when I realised where my zone of genius lies. And that it what I'm doing now and I'm super excited about it.

What I do.

I have different levels in my business, but what you might be most interested in is that I help people who are starting out, and I map everything out with them. I also help people who are kind of stuck in the middle to become more efficient and to re-evaluate. I create plans and give amazing tips born out of my extensive experience – from online to offline ideas, how you can develop your business, what is missing, how you can get more traction. I also help with the mindset side of running a business.

Check me out! www.christinemeansbusiness.com

I also offer travel experiences for entrepreneurs who are at a certain level. On these experiences we talk about streamlining, teams, Imposter Syndrome (because it never goes away), etc. It's for more seasoned entrepreneurs who love to travel and talk about business without being judged and knowing that the other person gets it, all while in a beautiful, new, inspirational setting.

I'm living my dream life and I want that for you too.

Your story.

Imagine you put the quote "let it go" on your Insta. Now, think of the film *Frozen*. Same message, world of difference, right? You're humanizing an experience and making it relevant to the person – this gives it emotional resonance. How smart is that?

Storytelling is the most human thing. That is why stories are so important in marketing because they are a bridge that connects one human to another.

Through stories, you don't simply communicate your expertise, you communicate meaning.

Now, you might be thinking: what if I don't have a story to tell? Believe me, I've been there. I didn't have a personal story the way many other creatives did. For my Sleep Like A Boss business, I didn't have sleep issues! I didn't have one of those anecdotes that lends itself so well to connecting with your clients: *I experienced x problem and found the solution.* But don't worry! Your heroine's journey doesn't have to be your own. You can take a client's story for example.

The goal with telling your story is to take someone on a **journey**. Your place in the story is being the expert that will help them get to the end. And, if you haven't reached the end of your own journey, be honest about that. Be transparent.

The relationship with your client should have a built-in love factor.

How to use your story.

Basically, you can use your story absolutely everywhere: on your website (the about page), in videos, social media feeds, Facebook ads, in talks / public speaking, books, webinars.

Now, when posting on your socials, think about how you can break up your story into snippets and snapshots. For example, "The moment I decided stuff needed to change." Take that and make it into a small story. Go deep into the details. Give a look behind the scenes, all about your process, etc. Social media is about developing relationships.

Ideally, you will have different stories around your core value about who you are. Create a story bank. Mine for stories in everyday life.

Important: Make sure your stories have a beginning, middle, and end.

Remember: Nobody wants to date the person talking nonstop about how hot they are. Apply that to social media too.

Be proud. Be real. Stories can heal.

5 steps to the perfect story.

1. The takeaway. The message you want to communicate. Your story should be evidence for the takeaway. Your message decides where to start and where to end your story.
2. The desire. What did you want that started your journey?
3. The challenge. What was hard?
4. The twist. What did you have to change to achieve your goal?
5. The shift. You've taken a new approach that gets you where you need to go.

What's Your Niche?

To Niche or Not to Niche

This chapter really depends on the type of business you have. Whether you work with people who have a certain condition or whether you provide a more general business. Personally, my niche is more value based, so I don't work like this, but have a read through this chapter and then decide for yourself. It's all about YOUR business.

First things first: Do you need a niche? The answer is simple. If you want to be easily found by Google, attract and market to your clients, then yes. That's all there is to it. BUT you don't have to go all out right from the start. Take it slow, let your niche develop. You can stay a bit more general in the beginning. You don't have to have it all figured out on day 1. And, even more importantly:

Give yourself permission to change.

Also, please understand a niche doesn't have to be a gender, age, or income situation. It can be a value or personality trait. Remember what I said about not investing in a branding coach at the beginning? The same applies here. A basic website will definitely suffice when you're starting out. The truth is, it's always easier to work on stuff behind the scenes than to go out and get clients. It's a mindset shift.

When I started out my niche was sleep. It was easy to write copy and easy for experts to find me. I am now Number 1 on Google. (*Want to know how I got there? Go to chapter 1.3.*)

Top tip: You can use Facebook ads to identify your clients. Use a general ad and see who Facebook targets. That's your client base.

Nugget of wisdom: Go with your name for your website (unless you have an awesome name like Sleep Like A Boss, of course).

Insider tip: A lot of people recommend creating your own client avatar, an exercise in generating your own client profile. BUT it limits you as to who your client can be. Problems with this technique are that you build a whole business on assumptions. You might alienate people unknowingly.

Remember my story for Sleep Like A Boss? I designed my business for women, but it attracts men too. And for my coaching business now, I thought I'd only work with coaches but actually I work with painters, interior designers. Who knew?

It really doesn't matter where your focus and your preferences are – let them shine like the lighthouse that you are. Believe me, it's so empowering.

Be a lighthouse.

How to Nail Down Your Niche Client Like a Pro!

Now, we've established a niche can be awesome. Let's dive a bit deeper into how to nail your niche and get those perfect clients.

What, exactly, is a niche? Let me tell you what it's not. It's **not** simply choosing a gender or country to focus on. Remember, you are competing with the ENTIRE INTERNET.

Think about it this way: When you fancy a meal out, which restaurant do you choose? The one that serves all the types of food in the world, or the one that specializes in the food you want?

Even if you are good at many things, it makes it so much easier and appealing for your customers if you specialize. Your clients don't know how everything in your business is connected. So, for your clients, the more different areas you work in the more confusing and chaotic it looks.

Meet people where they are without overwhelming them.

What I see happening a lot is that right after their training people use a lot of jargon to feel legit, but it's confusing to your clients. Instead, describe your business in a way that other people can relate to.

Now, when you start out, niching might feel a bit fake because you are adapting to the language of your clients. That means, describing your business in a way that other people can relate to, rather than the way you see it and rather than what you were taught in your training. That language can be really alienating. You. Don't. Need. To. Impress. Anyone.

If you speak like your client, that will connect with them. **Preaching down is not going to work.**

Nailing your niche client as a health coach.
A case study

The problem: adult acne.

The question: What does that person google? "How to deal with adult acne" OR "Solutions for acne." NOT: "health, wellness, nutrition." Right?

Let's say this person finds two websites of health coaches. One says: I help you uncover healing opportunities and improve health and wellness.

The other says: I help women in their 30s get clear skin naturally.

Which do they choose? No brainer! They choose the second. And again don't worry if you specify an age you will still have teens and 20 year olds and men reach out. If you can't meet people where they are, they're not going to pay attention.

How do people think about what they need? That's how you need to word your pitch.

Something a lot of people worry about is whether they will push people away by niching. You know what, that's okay, **the right clients will find you**. And, if people like you they will still contact you, even if you're not marketing to them. It's just NOT TRUE that you will have fewer clients when you niche. This is something I really want you to remember. Niching also makes your messaging clearer, and clearer messaging attracts clients **because they understand what you're saying.** Bonus: It also attracts people looking for experts, e.g., PR agencies, journalists needing quotes, etc.

Still not sure how to nail down your ideal client? Follow these fail-proof steps.

1. What are your values? Just remember your values.

I want clients who are like me.

Even if your client profile is super clear in your head, you might attract different people. I was marketing towards women, like, completely to women. My website actually said, "for women who can't sleep." And I still attracted men! Mostly, men in their 50s and 60s. Now, I mean, my good looks might have something to do with it. But seriously, you just never know. And you might shift. You might naturally attract people that you were not expecting to connect with.

Your niche will change with you and your business.

2. What is their problem? Please, please remember that making people aware of a problem they have, legitimatizing it, and showing them you understand is not the same as shaming them. AKA making them feel like a loser because they have that problem. If you struggle with this, look at forums to see what people are looking for. Consider yourself a nosy barista. Check Reddit. Hashtags. It can be funny but still be a problem. It needs to seriously rub them the wrong way. Otherwise, people are not going to pay big bucks for it, right? What is impacting people's jobs? Their focus, physical performance, looks? Their bottom line? Their relationships? What causes them embarrassment?

Example: I work with beginner entrepreneurs, setting up their business and providing the steppingstones for them to follow. It can be so overwhelming at the beginning, if you have someone to give you the steps from A-Z, or tell you which steps you're missing, all of the sudden everything becomes clear. And sometimes, these steppingstones get mixed up a bit, so that's when I also help people who are already further down the business road. It's my job to realign the message. And it doesn't have to be straightforward, it all depends on the individual and their business.

Interested in how I do it? Check my services section on my website out!

https://www.christinemeansbusiness.com

3. What is their desire? What do people actually want? This desire has to be related to the problem. Emotions come in really useful here: vanity, pride, happiness, etc. People base decisions on emotions, not logic. So, appeal to that.

Think of that friend who is always stressed about money. They still buy expensive treats, right? There's something about the shoes or whatever that makes them feel a certain way that is more valuable to them than healthy food.

These are the magic bullets: **Desire, feeling, emotion**.

You can also use scenarios people recognize – from films or TV, for example.

You should always only promise something that you know you can deliver. You have to be really realistic when it comes to the time frame. One really important point to make here is that I don't promise my clients to finish in 60 days, 90 days, whatever, even a year. I know it's a lot of work, life happens. Obviously, the time frame is collapsed so much through my help. It would take so much longer if you strike out on your own. It's so important to be honest when thinking about desire.

For my clients, desires are: work when they want to, have a good income for themselves, their family, emergencies, early retirement, doing something honest that they love, not having to work all the time, not being stressed. All these things are doable!

Sometimes people don't know what they need. Think back to my lighthouse metaphor. The little boats don't always know what they need. They might have a feeling, but they're not sure until they hear about it, see it, or read about it. And then it clicks for them. But remember, never shame anyone into something! Instead, make them aware of the gap they have.

The amazing thing is: When you know who you're talking to, you don't have to ask yourself what content to create. It'll come naturally. All you have to do is think these are the people **I really want** to help vs these are the people I think **need** my help.

Christine's Global Impact.

Obviously, you want to help as many people as possible and the way to do that is to include PR in your business.

For me, I focus on PR globally. Taking over the world, baby! Think global impact – I call it impact with integrity. It really puts you on a different stage. You're seen differently.

So, what does this entail? Media appearances such as TV or podcast interviews, being interviewed for online or offline magazines, guest blogging and expert appearances. This means that you will have to focus on pitching for these outlets for a certain amount of time. You have to be really focused, but it's fun, and you make good connections.

Don't be afraid to borrow other people's audiences through their podcasts, blogs, etc.

BUT always create your own content for your website as well. Google is the best referral partner you have.

Top tip: Don't focus heavily on one platform. If that gets shut down, you still need to have a business.

www.christinemeansbusiness.com

Biz Bomb

3 Steps to your (health coach) niche

Step 1: Figure out how to address your clients. Hormone imbalance? Not obvious what that means. But if you say fatigue, tiredness, etc., that's clearer.

Step 2: Hone your message. Use everyday language, not coded language (no 'empower,' 'take your health to the next level'). People are not always aware what their problem is.

Step 3: Your tagline. I help [target audience] to [your business] so that [goal].

Site tagline: get specific about what you do. E.g.: Sleep expert and coach for adults.

Your Brand Message: How to Talk to Your Niche so They Will Listen

You've nailed your niche; you've found your ideal client. Now, how best to talk to them?

I never made so much money as when I stepped into my messaging. Messaging is kind of scary because everything is part of it: your voice, body language, the way you dress, your aura, vibe, makeup, hair. And, of course, the obvious: writing, blogging, etc.

Show up for your ideal client.

Live and breathe your messaging every day. That doesn't mean you have to be perfect. *Phew, right?* I mean, I love dressing up, but I also love not wearing makeup and having bird-nest hair (I still look amazing, naturally, ha! Check me out on Insta for those glam just-rolled-out-of-bed stories: @bychristine_hansen).

Don't use stock photos on your feed or quotes that you privately don't agree with. People see through that stuff REALLY QUICKLY. But sometimes you do have to fake it (*hello filters*), just a teeny, little bit. It is about CURATING but also it has to be a part of YOU. **You are your brand**. Really investigate who you are.

Not everyone is happy admitting to themselves who they really are. You might be lazy, antisocial, a horrible person (I'm joking, I'm joking). But if you put those parts out in the open, other people who are like that will resonate. Introverts are having a huge movement right now whereas a few years ago being an introvert was basically a nice way of say you were a weirdo. Of course, who you show up as online is not the complete you. That's not possible. **Think of it as creating an avatar of yourself using key pieces of your personality.**

Me, I'm really bossy (my partner can attest, in fact, he's the one who told me that I am *shock and horror on my end*), but I'd NEVER put that on camera and especially not when I'm talking to clients. HOWEVER: you can take those slightly negative things and give people a peek. Write about it on your blog, for example. Then all the other amazing, bossy people or people who know they need a truth telling bombshell from time to time will want to hire you.

Now, here comes the bad news. Even if you have your niche carved out, there will still be ten people on the first page of Google who do **exactly the same** as you. But it's okay! Because when people stalk you and the ten others, they will connect with the person they can relate to the most. And hopefully that is you! And the only way they can connect is when you show who you are.

And if they don't connect with you, then you will probably not want to work with them anyway!

Top tip: Ask yourself how you want people to feel when others come into contact with your brand. So, if you teach meditation, for example, you want your brand to be calm, not chaotic. Take me, I can be super grumpy, like I'm the queen of grumpiness, but that's not something I show when I'm working with my clients or in videos. In practice, that means I don't do videos when I'm grumpy – even if there's a deadline.

Insider tip: Nobody needs to actually know who you are imagining creating your content for.

Categorize.

We humans are obsessed with categorizing. You can tie everything back to a problem or a topic and that's exactly what you should do. Make sure that your approach is translated into your voice, your visuals, who you are, etc. So, if you're someone who is a harsh person, don't be afraid to be harsh in your messaging. Plus, it's so much less exhausting if you can just be yourself. And if you're being interviewed, for a podcast for example, make sure it's still you even if the interviewer has a very different style.

When I talk about messaging, I literally mean it's
EVERYWHERE.

Time for a reality check.

There are some of us who are entrepreneurs AND great at building our business AND okay (or even great) at putting ourselves out there. And then there are the intrapreneurs who are also great at building a business but not so great at putting themselves out there. If that is you, consider whether having your own online business is the right choice, or whether partnering with someone else or going into another person's business might be a better fit.

And that's totally okay! You can learn how to show up but if it doesn't feel like you, just remember that there are other options. It's all about recognizing your strengths and weaknesses.

Top tip: If you're working with a web designer on your webpage, DON'T tell them to go to other people's pages and to model yours on those. You're not the same person, and it won't fit. This is why it's crucial to know who you are when branding (*see chapter 1.1*).

TOOLBOX

The best website to inspire your branding

Take my brand: Christine Means Business. For me, that stands for efficiency and elegance.

For your branding process, figure out your values, as well as the tone of what you stand for.

Insider tip: Go to creativemarket.com and, in the search bar, type in words that you identify with your values. The search engine will come up with different fonts and themes that you can use for your brand.

Starting from a point of value is much more efficient than to consider what is pretty.

Go Big

How to Book Media Appearances
(AND GET FEATURED ON TV!)

Let's get real. Getting featured is a dream. Not only for your business, but for your own self-worth. Visibility gets you credibility, and credibility gets you clients. All of that also makes you feel amazing about yourself. It's a win-win! If this is something you've always wanted (and why wouldn't you?), pour yourself a glass of red (or tea or coffee), and grab a comfy seat. I'll tell you how to get into magazines, onto the radio, and even on TV if that's your wheelhouse (it's definitely mine).

Start local. Dream big.

When I was first starting out with my business Sleep Like A Baby, I organized an on-location launch at a local café here in Luxembourg. I sent out press releases to local media and online platforms, which gave me media coverage and my first feature. Amazingly, people were interested in the topic! Leading on from that, I got 4-6 media features in my first year. I also made sure to be active on social media.

Now, for my next business – Sleep Like A Boss – I needed to step up (like a boss). I knew I only wanted high-end clients. I took

Selena Soo's course "Impacting Millions," in which I learned exactly where to look for media exposure. It took me around 3 months of pitching A LOT until I struck gold. And I mean, a lot. Every other day, I sent a pitch. I pitched podcasts, magazines, websites – everything from tiny to big. And in those 3 months, I was featured in *Brides* magazine, *Reader's Digest*, *The Huffington Post*, and *Elite Daily*. In fact, I became a regular contributor to *The Huffington Post*.

After those first three months, my website ranked pretty high. Now, if people google "sleep expert adults" I come up as number 1 or 2. And, because I already have those media credentials, people trust that I am a good source for other journalists. And everything just snowballs from there. I've had weeks where I've been featured in *The New York Post* on Monday, *The Independent* on Thursday, on Luxembourg's national TV on Friday, and on Saturday flown into Paris to appear on French TV.

When you're starting out, throw yourself out there. Go to your local newsagent and check the back of magazines for the name of the editor. Then write a competent (!) email to them asking to contribute. (See the example pitch template below.) That method got me into a high-end Belgian print magazine.

When you're launching your business, do everything you can to be a local sensation, and the magic will happen.

Insider top tip:

Now, here's an insider tip worth its weight in gold: I used to have a collaboration with a mattress company. I would freelance for them. They had an amazing PR team that works with one of the biggest PR companies worldwide (think the Williams sisters, UNICEF, etc.). As the sleep expert of this mattress company, I piggybacked all of their expertise and resources. When they had a campaign, they used me in their quotes as a consultant; so, when a reporter had a question, they connected them with me. I talked to the press and got the visibility. That TV appearance for which I was flown to Paris? I got that through them.

Your guide to the perfect pitch.

- When you're starting out, try pitching absolutely everywhere.
- Check. The. Guidelines. Some outlets want a complete story with images (e.g., mindbodygreen.com), others need just a pitch.
- Pitch 3-5 ideas at once.
- Some places don't take pitches at all because they have regular contributors. BUT you can try pitching those regular contributors directly! (I got into Forbes that way.)
- Do your research to see what their audience wants, what their voice is, etc.

- The biggest mistake people make? Their pitch is too long. Be short, be sensational.

Top tip: When you pitch, everything has to be above the fold: that means, when the editor clicks on your email, the most important stuff has to be visible straight away without needing to scroll.

Disclaimer: things have changed a LOT since 2016! Online magazines are flooded with pitches so make sure you follow their guidelines precisely and don't be discouraged when it takes a while.

The Pitch.

Start with your name, move into your elevator pitch (use flattery if you're pitching a podcast), then include your 3-5 bullet points – making sure you have catchy headlines. Mention that you're open to changes: if you need anything else, do let me know. Namedrop those features (with links) if you have them. Sign off. Then, right at the bottom, that's where you put your bio.

Podcasts.

An excellent place to pitch is podcasts. People who subscribe to podcasts are usually big fans of the topic discussed, so it's a more intense environment and your pitches should be more in-depth. Podcasters love to be flattered. So, get to know their programme and tell them what you love about it. The amazing thing: podcasts are evergreen, and people can find you years later.

Extra: when you appear on a podcast, create an opt-in on your page just for the podcast: a separate page on your website that is linked from the podcast, and that directly addresses the people coming from the podcast. Create that all-important personal connection.

Want to get on TV?

That's why you're reading this chapter, right? You want to get on TV. Of course, you do.

Practice on Facebook Live first if you're nervous. Be a guest on other Facebook Lives. Then, start with a small station, a local channel, or an online channel.

If you can collaborate with a company that has a great PR team, it's the most amazing thing. BUT: you must be a good fit and you must get along (like me and my mattress company). Remember that you might have to sign an exclusivity contract for about 6 months at a time. But you get paid for it! And that's what business is all about, right?

Still unsure if pitching is for you?

You don't have to be established before you pitch. I started pitching without anything under my belt. Be brave and go for it.

If you haven't been featured anywhere before, don't worry, and don't mention it.

With some sites, such as HARO (see the Toolbox), the quicker you are the more successful you'll be. I've even sent people a voice memo instead of writing emails. Play by the rules (until you don't need to anymore). Only once you've got some experience and connections can you experiment with your approach.

You don't have to try and get on national TV if that's not your jam. Start with local workshops and focus on local audiences, get on local radio. The most important thing is that you're comfortable with your approach.

Top Tip: Pitch your local media in the summer, that's when the summer slump happens, and they have much less to report on.

When it comes down to it, pitching is an amazing strategy to generate more income and get those sweet clients. It's a credibility marker. Having those fancy logos on your page gives you authority. It's much less work than hustling for clients. But remember, you do need to be comfortable being visible and being out there.

In the end, it doesn't even matter how many people see you, it's about getting that credibility.

Oh, and while we're talking about credibility? My podcast this book is based on? It was featured in Forbes.

TOOLBOX

Tool of the day: HARO

www.helpareporter.com

A free platform on which reporters ask for experts. You can pitch to reporters and get featured. HARO helped me get my first steps to visibility.

See also:

SOURCEBOTTLE

www.sourcebottle.com

BRAINZMAGAZINE

www.brainzmagazine.com

For podcasts, see also:

matchmaker.fm

podbooker.com

vurbl.com

My podcast booking agency:

Podcastbookers.com

Secret tip: Check out my interview with Nick Wolny on my blog. He's a superstar on writing and content creation!

https://www.christinemeansbusiness.com/what-is-content-
and-why-writing-is-important-for-your-online-business-with-
nick-wolny/

Your Digital Home

Can Simplifying Your Website Get You More Clients? With Jessica Freeman

First things first. You don't have to have a website to start. Say whaaat? Yes, really!

If you feel overwhelmed, you can start without one. BUT (you knew there'd be a 'but' right?): Ultimately, your website will be all about your messaging and tapping into building your authority.

Cool stuff you can put on your page.

Media logos mean I've been in these publications, podcasts, I got these results for clients. All of this helps build trust because it says you've been trusted by other people. Places I've been in? *Entrepreneur, Forbes, The Guardian, Vogue, Business Insider,* TEDx, *The Independent....*

All of this builds your credibility.
And you know what credibility gets you?
Exactly: Clients.

Of course, you can share those things on Insta and on other socials too. But there are people who need to see a website to believe in you, to know that you're legit. And guess what? There are actually still people who are not on social media!

Jessica's 2 amazing fixes that can immediately make a website better.

1. Simplify your website. It can feel overwhelming to have too much content for visitors. Figure out what you really want people to do. Don't give visitors more than 3 options or calls to action on a page. That means: no more than 3 buttons, links, thumbnails, etc. (not counting your menu button).

Think about: What's the next best step you want your visitor to take? And that can change from quarter to quarter. So, imagine you want to build your email list in one quarter because in the following quarter you want to launch your course.

It's a simple matter of changing the button to direct to this page or that page, so you don't have to redesign your website.

2. Don't have too many options in your navigation menu. Essentials: 4-5 links in the menu:

- **1: Your about section**. Seems pretty explanatory but actually I have a whole section on that (*see the BizBomb in Chapter 2.3*).

- **2: Your services**. (You can add dropdowns to your services. Dropdowns are your friend!) There is no right or wrong about having all your services on one page or on separate pages. But if you list them on separate pages, you must make it worth people's while to visit those pages!

- **3: Your resources page**. Add any affiliate links. What are things you could suggest to your audience? Books, tools, etc.

- **4: Your links**. Add links to your blog, podcast and/ or your YouTube channel. This section can live underneath the resources tab in the dropdown menu or on a separate page.

- **5: Your dedicated testimonials page**. Especially if you've been in business for a while – this is a fantastic feature. You can sprinkle testimonials around your website, as well as have them on a separate page. Then, when you're talking to a potential client you can direct them to that page.

- **6 (extra): Your media or press page**. Podcasts you've been on, blogs, publications, public speaking. Here is where you brag, big time!

Christine's top tip: Now, I've been keynote speaker on the topic of sleep lots and lots of times. However, on the topic of business development – what my second business is all about – not so much, yet. (Get those invites coming, people!) BUT giving keynotes is still a skill I have developed, regardless of the topic, so I can add all those sleep talks to my media page of my business coaching website. See? Don't limit yourself, you can use past experiences.

Jessica's one thing that is a no go for your website:

One thing you should be really wary of is having too many colours and fonts. Apply what Jessica calls **the rule of 2**: Two fonts, two colours. Simple.

Yes, I know you might have three favourite colours – but, believe me, in this case simple is good.

Having 2 colours and 2 fonts helps you look more cohesive overall. It's simply professional. There are easy steps to make your website more uniform. For example, have all your buttons be the same colour. (Save all your other hot colours for your socials.)

Now, if you see someone's website with 5 colours and it looks amazing, chances are that they used a designer!

Top tip: I find fonts so, so hard. Get someone else to do it if you can. (By the way, that is my motto anyway; **if you can pay for help, do it**. *Read more about that in Chapter 2.4*)

How to choose fonts.

- Use Google: search for "best font combinations" to figure out which 2 best go together.
- If you're using one serif font (those are the fonts with those curly things, e.g., Times New Roman) add one sans serif font (they have no deco, e.g., Helvetica and Arial).
- You can choose to use just one font family: e.g., Montserrat. So, you can use headers in Montserrat Bold, the body in Montserrat Regular, etc.
- You can also use the same font for everything and use your two colours to separate; so, have your heading in one colour and then the main body of text in black.

Getting people to find you.

How do we get people to find us? What you're looking for is conversion: That means, somebody coming to your website and doing one action. That could be to book a call, sign up to your email list, etc.

The best way to get people onto a website is CONTENT. CONTENT. CONTENT. In addition: Optimizing your content so you show up on Google (SEO, baby. *Check it out in Chapter 3.1*).

However, don't overdo SEO. Say, if you used all the words suggested through SEO strategy your text most likely won't make sense anymore. Instead, one simple thing you can do is to optimize your page titles. Often, people have their home page and it's called "home" or something like "Jess creatives." Unless someone actually searches "Jess creatives," you're not going to show up. (And who is going to search for that? Unless they know you, obviously.)

Check what settings your platform has. For example, WordPress, Yoast, All-In-One SEO give you an option on your page where you can optimize your title. Optimize it for search without it showing on the front of your website. Other platforms have an SEO setting for each page.

What are people searching for?

Examples could be: Your city plus "health coach". Or your city plus "women's hormone health coach". **Be really specific.** The more niched the better.

A **good thing to know**: Meta descriptions. Those are the little texts you see under search result in Google; a summary of what's on the page. Don't just list words in your meta description: e.g., city, health coach. You want to speak naturally: "Hey, I'm an Atlanta-based health coach. I help women with…"

So, you have your title and description, and you do that for each page. You want to make sure they're different for each page. Use variations on your titles. Very important: Make sure the title ACTUALLY reflects what's on the page.

2. Running Your Business

Section 2

RUNNING YOUR BUSINESS

When you start an online business and you start googling launches and courses, it's inevitable that you will come across the idea that you should have a group programme and a course and how to launch it. Very often with the 'build it and they'll come' mentality. If you are lucky then you will also be told you're supposed to make people aware of this course. Probably via social media or email. You have a launch period where you make even more noise for your product, you open your cart where people can buy it, and you're sorted. People have amazing testimonials who've done this.

Well, let me tell you, I tried this.

LOADS.

I tried it with my health coaching business, Sleep Like A Boss, and my launches were always a disaster. They never ever turned out the way I was hoping for – they always underperformed. Because when people don't know you exist, then they can't buy from you! Also launching is not for everyone. It just doesn't suit every personality, and when you don't enjoy it it shows and influences the outcome.

So, I didn't do any launches for three years. And then with my business coaching business I decided, what the hell, I'm going to give it another go. And I did it all. I hired a launch strategist, mindset coach, event planner. And even though I implemented everything perfectly, with Facebook ads, invested a lot of money, it totally failed once again. I figured out a super important lesson for me, which is **to listen to my gut**.

I didn't feel great about launching. Another lesson I learned was that my soulmate audience is just not people who buy small price items. It's not the way I present myself or my products, offers, or services. So, there's a huge disconnect there. The takeaway is that launching small products really isn't for everyone unless you have a well thought out funnel that does match your character. (Again, have a look at Allie Bjerk for this). Don't get too convinced by the promises of a big launch. Make sure it actually is aligned with the business you have. Then, again, it might be for you. Check in with yourself, with your business, and decide what's right for you.

That means, many of the chapters in this section on launching are based on interviews with the experts who have had success in this, because it's just not my thing. But it might be yours!

Whatever you decide, if you do launch make sure to do the prep and check whether what you're launching is what people want.

Setting up Your Business for Success

Launching a Programme

Here we go: You've got your story, you've got your niche, now you need a programme to actually start teaching people or informing them more about what you're good at, right? But this is not only for the coaches among you. Having a programme, having a methodology – that is, a process of how YOU do things – is invaluable. Even if you are an artist or a creator. Your way of thinking, your process is valuable. It's the ticket to fame! It's the thing you will become KNOWN for.

Launching a programme.

Establish a methodology you become known for: A signature programme that delivers a result. That methodology is your ticket to freedom. The way to come up with it? Identify your ideal client (*see Chapter 1.2*). Identify the steps you teach and implement over and over. Package those into a framework. My Impact with Integrity method, for example, is: Branding, Pricing & Packaging, Email & Tech, Content Creation & Distribution, and finally, Global Outreach. Those are the 5 pillars every business should entail. When you have a launch, you're putting an event around your programme. While launching is one of the strategies to grow business, don't rely only on it; you need to get clients year-round.

The idea to take away here is to have mainstay: Create the methodology you become known for.

Create the method you're the expert for.

Concrete steps to take before launching your programme.

1. Build a methodology. What are the fundamentals your ideal client needs to get results?
2. Beta test that methodology, i.e., let people know it's unfinished and a test, often at a reduced price and not as professionally produced. Either with a group or one-on-one. The important thing is that you beta-test at all. It doesn't matter if you start with a group or one-on-one. You just need an x number of people to have gone through your methodology **to make sure it works**. That's your experience. Those are your first 5 clients.
3. Only then think about the model you want to use. It also alleviates so much pressure to be perfect.
4. Collect ALL. THE. Feedback. You can use feedback later on. You can then change your programme or not, it's up to you.

Top tips for group programmes:

- Okay, you've got your methodology, now you want to probably create a group programme. Here are some tips:
- Decide whether you want to launch sporadically or whether you want the programme to be evergreen, i.e., have people enrol all year round.
- A group programme doesn't need to have a hundred people, a group of 4 or 5 people is just as valid!
- Organise weekly group calls (it doesn't matter where people are in the course).
- Offer an additional level of support: one-on-one, for an extra upgrade fee
- The hot times to launch: spring and autumn.

Magic tip: A programme doesn't sell. What sells is your ability to identify the person who needs it. Then, connect the programme to the person's problem. Boom.

Biz Bomb

A Launch Strategy to get you Sales FAST

Credit to: Amie Tollefsrud from Rebelle Nutrition.

Okay, so you've got your business up and running, you've got your niche down, you've got an amazing course or product. Now you need to launch it into the world.

The most important thing with any launch is URGENCY. You need to give people the impetus to act quickly.

If somebody tells you that their product is available forever, you can get it now or in ten years, are you likely to rush to buy it? In fact, you might never buy it.

What you need to do when you launch is to give people deadlines, so they are under pressure to act. And you need to give them a reason to **take action quickly**. When I have a new programme, a course (not an evergreen course), I have people sign up for a waitlist, or a VIP list. I tell them: Get on the list so you'll know when the course becomes available, and I'll offer discounts and bonuses you won't get anywhere else.

Then, 2 weeks before the launch, I send an email with the date – as a VIP you'll get early access. The VIPs get access 24 hours before the general public, and, if you take action quickly, you'll get a bonus on top.

Another thing you can do is say: The first person who signs up will get a full refund. What? Yes, it totally works! Those who didn't get the course for free still get a big discount.

How to Create Your First Digital Product

Digital products.

You can get value out of something solely digital. You're packaging all of your knowledge into one product that you can use as a complimentary tool in multiple ways. One-on-one, group coaching, freebie, a membership site...

Go from a freebie to a $500 product.

By having a digital product, you are making a difference AND money without you physically being there. That frees up space in life and business. It opens up a creative space. You don't have to talk about the same topics over and over. Also, it means you can work with the people you really want to. If someone isn't the right fit, you can direct them to your digital product and possibly work with them personally later on. PLUS: You get extra clout; **you're choosing and deciding who to work with.**

You can package all of your training packages into digital products. Even my one-on-one clients go through my digital products. It makes no sense for me to repeat the same information over and over. Clients give positive feedback on this because they can sit with the content and reflect, and I don't worry about leaving stuff out. AND your clients can always refer back to the content.

One piece of content is several income streams. And even more amazing: your coaching calls can really be about coaching rather than learning.

How to know what digital products to create.

Ask yourself: What kind of content do my clients like? Who am I creating for? (What's your niche? *See Chapter 1.2*) What is the immediate problem your audience is experiencing right now and what stage of the problem are they in?

For example, if you're a coach helping people to set up digital products, you might offer a beginning stage: how to set up, a middle: creating and designing product, and a final stage: marketing and selling products. Each of those stages can be individual products or can be made into a bundle.

The different phases of a digital product

1. idea phase, 2. creation phase, 3. packaging phase, 4. marketing and enrolment phase.

Map out how long it takes you to create. Give yourself time. Otherwise, you'll burn out. Say you want to do an 8-module course, you create 3 modules ahead of time and then pre-sell it. Then, you can work on a module a week.

Even if a full course doesn't sell, you can break it up and sell as master classes.

Types of digital products.

- Audio

Audio courses, mediation series, exclusive podcasts, audio Q & A with clients or just give the answers. (Anytime you can show yourself teaching is a win.) Audio is low maintenance, maybe you don't feel confident on video (yet!). Go to my YouTube channel for tips: https://www.youtube.com/c/ByChristineHansen/videos.

- Video

Video, online courses, master classes, workshops, webinar, FB Live or IGTV Live series can all be packaged! Consider tiny offers, create an ad for a tiny offer, straight to a sales page with a no-brainer price, instead of a lengthy funnel. (Again, check out Allie Bjerk's Tiny Offer Lab® and *See Chapter 3.2 on how to create an amazing funnel.*)

- Texts

eBooks, training manuals, workbooks, meal plans, challenges, planners, info graphics, journal prompts.

- Experiential digital products

Something to do, quiz, fitness video, implementation guides with video.

Top tip: SEO research is so important to make sure you're not wasting time with creating stuff people don't want (*See Chapter 3.1*).

How to sell your product:

1. Package it first. It needs to be housed somewhere. A template or checklist could be in Google

Drive or Dropbox. For online courses with several modules, check out content delivery systems (e.g., Podia, Teachable, Thinkific). http://www.christinemeansbusiness.com/podia

2. Add it to a sales funnel.

3. Drive traffic to it.

Use the content you have and break it down.

BOOKBOX

Carmine Gallo, *The Presentation Secrets of Steve Jobs*

Client Management

Biz Bomb

What To Do When Your Client Gets Stuck

1. Forget about worrying why your clients are not getting results! Self-sabotage is okay (everyone does it), but it needs to be fixed. Your job is to find out when it is happening.

    Make sure you know who to refer your client to when there is a problem that is outside of your expertise.

It's a story of mind and body. Take time to create space for your clients. This creates trust and motivation.

2. Boundaries, boundaries, boundaries: Write down boundaries in your client agreement, when to expect notes, etc. *(go to Chapter 2.2 for more)*. I highly suggest getting a legal advisor going through your client agreement even if you are using a template given to you. It will help any future drama and gives you a lot of peace of mind.

3. Identify if there is a gap in what your clients are telling you and not telling you. Emotional stress is a big factor that needs to be identified. Remember that building a business is a rollercoaster of feelings.

4. Know when to refer to a specialist. A psychologist, psychiatrist, hypnotherapist, whatever. Build relationships to practitioners so you have easy referrals.

Biz Bomb

The ONE Thing You Should Never Leave Out of Your Client Contract

Okay, let's get serious. Contracts are vital to set out boundaries and expectations, explain how interactions work, etc. It is imperative to get them right. Better to go overboard with what you include than to leave stuff out. You can always make an exception. But if it's not in your contract, you **have to give a refund** when demanded. Naturally, your contracts will evolve over time.

The one thing you always need: **the absence rule**. Let's say you have a 6-month course. Some people might fall off the track, they'll cancel, go off the radar. You need a rule that says if you're absent for a certain amount of time (say, 3 months), you need to pay this to re-start the package. What you really don't want is for people to just show up years later and want to continue! You might not have time, your prices might (should!) be higher, etc.

Important: Stick with your absence rule, even if someone has a sob story. Sure, you can always make exceptions if you must – but the bottom line is always:

You're running a business, baby !

Biz Bomb

Your About Section

The about page is the most visited page on your website, and the page people spend the most time on. The biggest mistake people make is that they write about themselves. I mean, it makes sense, it's called the ABOUT page. BUT in the end, people don't really care about you. (Sorry!)

They don't care about your story. They care about **how** your story can help **them**. What have you learned that can help them? They are about to invest money with you – they don't really want to know about you. How can you justify their investment?

People can find out more about you through your social media or blog posts. Your about page should only be about **how you can benefit them**.

I see a lot of about pages – especially for health coaches – where they talk about their own journey. BUT what you need to do is this: every time you say something about yourself, add why it benefits others. So, when you start with your journey – I felt crappy about this and this – state how this benefits your clients because you understand where they're coming from and how to motivate them. You know what worked for you and what will work for them.

Every step in your personal journey, you need to explain why that helps your future client.

You story doesn't actually have to be about the same journey your client goes through. I built Sleep Like A Boss even though I was never an insomniac. My about story would not have been interesting to clients. Back then, the about section on my website had nothing about me! A little bit about my certifications, that was it. It was all about how I strive to help people.

Biz Bomb

You don't Need to be in IT to Set up a Website

I love domains! I have so many. Obviously, those for my websites: christinemeansbusiness.com and sleeplikeaboss.com, but I also have domains for various other sleep-themed nirvanas:

sleepretreat.vip
theholisticsleepinstitute
womensdivinesleepsummit

Confused about terminology? Go to the **glossary** at the beginning of this book!

You don't need to keep them forever but when a golden idea strikes act fast.

My tip would be to try and get everything at one service for your domain and hosting. There are so many options. You can go with one-stop shops, such as Squarespace or Wix, or use a system such as WordPress that is essentially a programme where you can use a builder to fully customize your website. I, personally, like WordPress because they do unlimited plug-ins for extra abilities, and they're constantly updated. With Squarespace or Wix you can only use what they provide. But they're also simpler to set up.

If you want to use WordPress: You get your domain at a hosting service (EasyDns, HostGator or I use: SiteGround, love it).

Step 1 Get your domain.

Step 2 Get your hosting.

Then you go into your back office (c panel) and add WordPress.

Tip: Wordpress.com is a blogging platform. Wordpress.org is the one to build a website. You want the latter.

If you're totally new – and this is something I've done – open a live chat and say: *Help, I've just bought this domain, how do I get hosting and website?* They will guide you through it, and even set it up for you.

Love my style and want to know the builder I use? Here you go: thrivethemes.com and elementor.com

Hiring People

Outsourcing and growing

What I teach my clients from the beginning is to set up your business so that you can easily hire people when you need them. As an online business, you don't have to invest in office space, which is fantastic. You can hire people from all around the world.

The way my business works is I create the main, raw piece of content, and then I have all the rest taken on by my team (*see more in Chapter 2.4*)

Read on to find out how to hire and fire the right people and where to find them!

Hiring the Right People for Your Small Business

There are two categories of hiring when you're running your own business. One, hiring freelancers. Two, hiring assistants.

Let's talk about freelancers. Generally, freelancers are employed as a one-off, which means they are often not as expensive to hire.

Where to find them? On places like Fiverr and Upwork (see next Chapter). BUT be careful that you're a good fit. You might have to explain a lot and that's ALWAYS a waste of time.

When hiring team members, it is absolutely vital to get it right. Bring people in earlier than you might think. The first VA (Virtual Assistant) I hired for $10/ hour to do my graphics couldn't take any initiative; she couldn't do everything I needed. You don't want to have to babysit your employees! More tips on that in a bit.

Definitions.

The VA. Virtual Assistant. They are there to take on those things that take time and that can be easily followed through instructions. Usually self-employed and working from a home office they are specialising in administrative services or simple graphic design. Typical tasks might include scheduling appointments, making calls, arranging travel, managing email accounts, designing graphics, organising things, pulling information, and setting up events.

The OBM. Online Business Manager. They are a step up from a VA, they know the ins and outs, delegate clients, know your marketing and content systems, and help you to optimize and organise. I have an OBM as well as virtual assistants because an OBM is paid more, and they are usually too sophisticated to do the work of a VA. The OBM manages an online business, that is, the daily operations so that the business owner does not have to. The OBM is the CEO's best friend. They project manage, manage operations, manage metrics and people.

My current assistant grew with me.

What can you outsource?

The truth? Pretty much everything except working with your clients and the first step of content.

- Client onboarding – my assistant takes care of that. So, when a client signs up with me, my assistant sends them the intake form, the scheduling, the contract, and the payment link. My assistant replies to prospective clients and schedules calls with me.

- Content creation: I create one video, my assistant delegates that to the team of freelancers who put it on Facebook, get it transcribed, put it in a blog post with graphics, on YouTube, Pinterest, Twitter, podcast, social media feeder (scheduled across the year). I hate doing those things, and she does it so much better. She also organises my Insta posts and graphics in general.

- Hashtag research: I hired someone to research hashtags for 15 bucks; they came up with around 200 hashtags I can use for my business. Even if you can do something but find it draining, free up that time and hire someone.

- Customer service is great to hire someone for. **If it's not the core of your business, if it doesn't need your face or voice, you can outsource it.**

Ask yourself what you're not good at – that's who you need to hire for.

Top tip: Take a month and make a list of what tasks could be done by someone else. For example, designing graphics is not something you have to do. The client sessions, yes, that is your job. A podcast interview? Also your job. But do you have to schedule the podcast interview? No, if you give your VA access to your calendar, they can do that. Pitching podcasts? You don't have to do that either.

Make two lists: one with the tasks you have to do, one with the tasks you can outsource.

Where to find people?

Reach out to your community. Check LinkedIn. University pin boards. Personally, I'm not a fan of Upwork: I had a bad experience with some dishonest people on there and lost $300. They didn't do the work and then disappeared, and I got no support from Upwork. But others had great experiences so research and decide for yourself.

Insider tip for Upwork: If you are paying someone per hour, make sure you limit the hours per week, otherwise it defaults to forty.

Questions to ask when hiring.

- Ask for references and Check. Up. On. Them.
- Make them record a video introducing themselves and send it to you.

- Give them a small task to do in the job description. (I.e., tell them to send their CV at a certain date and a certain time. If they can't handle that: buh bye)
- Make sure to have Standard Operation Procedures (SOP) in place, i.e., tutorials or an onboarding manual showing people what they need to do so you don't have to go through that.

I have a library of tutorials so when I need to hire someone new (I had to hire two new assistants when my existing ones became pregnant), it's straightforward for the new hire to work their way in.

- Be clear about expectations. This is so important! What does the position entail? What is your communication style? And what are clear results you expect? I.e., audience growth, the number of certain tasks done, etc.
- Ask questions where you can gauge whether they will be able to make decisions on their own. The worst thing is if you have to micro-manage them. You want self-sufficient people. My assistant, Tamara, offered to tidy up my system when I gave her access to it. I was like hell, yes!
- Have clear boundaries: when they get paid for what in which amount of time.
- Set expectations of how you want to work with your people.

- Take your time checking someone out, do a trial period, like 30 days, before hiring. Make sure they're following your expectations.
- Hire and fire quickly.

Top tips: Your business needs to be their baby as much as yours. And tell them how you appreciate them. Or if something bothers you.

Hire early before you're desperate, otherwise you'll make bad decisions out of that desperation.

TOOLBOX

There are handy tools you can use to check how your employees log their time.

Hubstaff: takes screenshots every few seconds.

Toggle: you can see in graphics what they've been working on.

Loom: records screens.

I would record myself doing stuff and my assistant could watch and copy. And then she created a log book (her own initiative). So now this logbook shows how to do everything, if ever I need a new assistant. Your assistant needs to be updating that manual, logbook, etc. Because if they leave, and the process isn't recorded, you're screwed.

Biz Bomb

You MUST Do This Before You Hire Anyone!

Whether you're hiring someone long term or short term, you need to be really, really, really, really clear on what you really want. This is the most important thing. You need to give super clear directions. Because: no one can read your mind. (*Thank goodness for that, euhem ...*)

If you have someone come in to build your website, you CAN'T just say: build me a website. Be specific. Contractors should also ask for direction. You need to know the outcome that you want. The contractor needs to know it too.

Example: Looking to hire a VA? Think of all the tasks that they're going to be doing and come up with procedures for each task and what you expect. Get an idea how long each task might take. Before you hire anyone, sit down and brainstorm what you need and want and what you're expecting the outcome to be.

The better you learn how to communicate, the better the result you'll get.

Tips From a CEO on How to Hire, Fire, and Build Culture in Your Small Business with Gina Michnowicz

As you're scaling quickly you might add people who are not the right people. They might have the right skills, and you might be under pressure to expand, but they're not a right fit for your culture. Even if they're remote. In the interview process, follow your gut.

If the spark isn't there don't hire them.

It's a mistake not to focus on the process and operational side of your business. Having that foundation is critical. **You need a process.**

89

Are you the culture?

As the CEO of your business, are you its culture? Culture is something you have to focus on, strategize on. It's a living, breathing thing. The CEO steers and role models the culture of a business. If I want everyone to be supportive, I need to be supportive of everyone. Accountability needs to start at the top. The CEO is the heartbeat and the brain. So, yes, you're the culture of your business. Add another notch to your amazingness!

Think of culture like a brand, it's a personality. What you want to focus on is really making sure you have actionable characteristics. I.e., where you want to be or what your values are. What do you want it to **feel** like?

Surround yourself with people who contribute to that. And get rid of the person who doesn't. Instead of company values, put out what you want to do to get to where you want to be. What you want it to feel like, what's the mission, the vision. And what does it take to get there?

How to fire an employee.

Less is more. When it's not a good fit, Gina says she tries to get the person to leave on their own accord. SMART.

Gina: "*I make their job one that they don't want. And I start hiring their replacement. Have conversations about how it's not working. Give them 30 days as a trial. Make sure you have key performance indicators, aka results so that there's no miscommunication.* "

Need to fire clients? Use the message: *We're just not a good fit.*

BOOK BOX

Daniel Coyle, *The Culture Code: The Secrets of Highly Successful Groups*

Find a leadership role daunting?

If you really don't think you can lead, hire someone who can. You can be the creative lead AND you can hire someone who is an expert to be a leader. Or you might just need a right-hand person!

Biz Bomb

How to Use Fiverr For Your Business

Fiverr is a website where you can hire freelance contractors. I use it for small copywriting projects, graphics, online invoices typed up into excel, podcast show notes, designers... Back in the day, all jobs started at five bucks. These days, most start at $20. You might not get the best quality, but it is more than enough to free up some time for you to get clients. You can either search for a gig or post for a gig. When you search, the same people will rank highly. So, I write very specific descriptions. Then you can hire them for a small job and tell them if it works out you will hire them on a retainer. I got my project manager from Fiverr, I have people helping me with YouTube, SEO, video editors. ALL THE THINGS.

Biz Bomb

Reasons Why You Need to Hire Help

Most creatives wait way too long to hire help. I say, you should hire someone at the 6-12 month mark in your business. I know what you're thinking. But I just started out myself. Right? Perhaps you're a perfectionist who can't let go of your business baby, let me tell you: that will be your downfall. If you have so much to do you won't have the space for your clients. If you think about it, in no successful company does the owner do everything!

If you struggle with hiring, ask yourself: what are you afraid of? Do you feel lazy, you're still a beginner, too big of an investment? Word of wisdom, my friend: it is an initial cost to outsource but because it enables you to focus so much more on being visible and delivering great services for your clients, it is the best way to grow your business successfully.

Here's the thing: You will not be able to grow, progress, or make money if you're trying to do everything yourself. Think about it this way: If you were starting a brick-and-mortar business, you would never do that without investment. So why is an online business different? Okay, you can start with much less, but just because the start is cheap doesn't mean you should run it cheaply.

You will stay stuck if you don't hire help.

Now, before you go allocate all your work to someone else from day one. Listen up. Initially, you MUST do all the things. Learn every aspect of your business because if you don't understand how it works, you'll get into trouble when you outsource. I only saw someone very recently post a very distraught comment in a group on how desperate they were because their VA left them and they had no clue how to run the business now.

People can take advantage of you so easily and overcharge for their services. But once you have a handle on everything and know what it is and how long it takes, that's when it's time to outsource.

There are so many things in your business you don't need to be doing and that don't make you money. The great thing is you can get help for little cost. And just imagine all the wonderful things you can do with your extra time! Go on holiday, browse (and buy) expensive lingerie, have long brunches with friends; in short, **live like a boss.**

Things you can outsource.

For a whole week or month, keep track of every single task you do in your business. Emails, customer service, content, socials, file, protocols. Time yourself to get an idea how long everything takes you. Then, put all of these tasks into two categories.

1. Tasks that **only you** can do.
2. Task you can **outsource**: Client onboarding, filing, scheduling, emails. Then figure out which you're the worst at and which you hate the most. Those are the ones to outsource.

TOOLBOX

App to track your time: Toggl

Money Matters: Getting clear on your offers

How to Price Your (Coaching) Packages

Right, let's get down to the money, shall we? Now, before you even start thinking about pricing hourly or whatever, you need to recognize the value you bring to your clients.

You should be confident in your knowledge and ability to help clients. After all, you got those certifications, you took courses, you have talent, and you've got the knowledge. The mere fact that people have found you shows that they are looking to invest for your type of service and willing to pay online prices. The price you charge will determine your success, portray your professionalism, and prove that you are LEGIT.

While this chapter is aimed at coaches, the principles can be applied to any online business.

What's in a coaching package.

What you include in your coaching packages should be clearly defined and simple. Lay out the expectations from the beginning so when you get to the pricing segment your potential client will understand exactly what they are paying for and will see the value for what they are paying. (*Check out Chapter 2.1 on how to create a digital product.*)

How much should I charge for coaching?

Let's look at the factors to consider (and not consider) when setting prices for your online coaching packages. Many other coaches will advise to base your prices upon who you are working with. For instance, if you are working with CEOs, you could charge more and if you are working with students then you won't be able to charge as much.

I call BS on this advice. Why would you assume what a certain clientele will spend? Spending and having is not the same thing. Just because someone has the funds doesn't mean they will prioritize spending it. And being willing to spend money on something someone finds valuable doesn't necessarily reflect their bank account.

Most people want a quick fix. Like in health, people are willing to pay money for quick fixes rather than spend time working out, learning how to eat well, or focusing on preventive care. *(Hello, plastic surgery versus ditching gluten and pounding the treadmill.)* With that in mind, pricing your coaching packages should focus on the value your package provides your clients.

The "actual" value of your package.

As I mentioned, people like a quick fix. **People don't buy coaching; they buy the outcome**. So, what outcome do you guarantee? Saving your clients time is your guarantee. Marketing your online coaching packages so that your ideal clients will save time is a crucial element to justifying your coaching prices. I call this outcome "time collapsing." The client will receive all the information they need in a one-stop shop without having to google months' worth of information on their own. You have all the info they need wrapped up in a pretty bow for them to have in just weeks, if not days. This allows your clients to get started on the path they seek and get on with their life.

Your clients are paying for you to save them time.

How to package your offers.

1. **Fee per session.** I have found this to be the least beneficial way to offer your coaching packages. This method leads to burnout, and you don't get paid if you don't have participants. Today's coaches can charge a whole hell of a lot more than old-school therapists as well, so charging by the session essentially leaves money on the table.

2. **Fee for a specific period of time.** This package works well if you set it up correctly. As a coach you know best how long it takes for a client to see results. Include time for follow up sessions and homework, and break your sessions up into six or 12 sessions over a three-to-six-month period. I advise not going over six months as

anything longer seems daunting, out of reach, and time consuming.

3. **Membership fees.** This packaging works well when you offer group sessions, however it is only truly successful when you have many people interested in your coaching package. Promoting this type of coaching package can only really be done if you have a substantial following.

4. **Fee based on results.** This is by far the best method for setting your coaching prices. Again, you know when the client will see results, so you base your package on the expected results. Provided the client follows all the steps, they are guaranteed to reach a certain outcome. You can charge very high for this type of package because you can guarantee the result. You should have a coaching contract that sets out all the expected lessons, templates, activities, etc. so the client knows exactly how to achieve the outcome he or she is paying for.

Things to consider.

Although the value and outcome of your coaching packages is number one, there are a few other factors to take into consideration when you set your fee.

- **Skills and experience**. If you are just starting out, you can charge your first five clients at a reduced rate. This way you can test how long it will take them to reach the desired result. You should be very clear that after the first five clients your prices will rise. After that, it is acceptable to raise your prices by 20% after every three new clients until you reach your ideal cost.

- **Testimonials**. Obviously, testimonials speak highly of your ability, so asking for these is essential once a client completes your package. The more testimonials and social proof you have from your past clients illustrates your competency and justifies your online coaching prices.

- **The actual value of your coaching packages**. How valuable is the transformation you precipitate to your clients? How much collapsed time are you granting your clients? Does your outcome promise money making if all the steps are followed to a T? Remember, you are selling the actual value of the outcome of your coaching packages, not the coaching itself.

- **What's included in your coaching packages.** The information that you provide to your clients should be considered when setting your coaching prices. Do you offer templates, bonus sessions outside of the package, or one-on-one mentoring? Facetime is golden in coaching packages, and the more tete-a-tete you can minister, the more your coaching fees will be deserved.

My top tip: Forget market research.

Don't do Facebook polls. Why in the world would you ask a group of strangers their thoughts on your pricing? You don't know their relationship with money and what they want to spend it on.

Don't ask friends. Have you ever seen the tryouts on American Idol of the kids whose parents told them they were great singers, when they in fact sound like nails on a chalkboard? That's essentially what your friends will tell you, "Yeah! I'd pay that!" But they actually wouldn't. They're just being nice.

DON'T google compare research. The fact is, it depends on where you live and your individual lifestyle, not the average salary of online coaches, that should help determine your coaching prices. Someone in New York City isn't going to charge the same as someone living in a rural area as their living expenses are much higher. This ties in with asking other coaches what they charge. You don't know what their lifestyle is like, if they need to make money to cover their bills, what their package offers, or if they undervalue their own expertise.

Let's get down to numbers.

In the past I have charged 800 euro for six sessions, and I found it harder to get the number of clients I needed than when I raised my price to 7.000 euros. Pricing too low may result in too many clients for you to handle or devalue your coaching package.

My rule of thumb is that a normal package should cost one-third of your monthly bills. So, say you need to make 10.000 per month, you would price your coaching packages at 3.000. Therefore, you would need at least three new clients per month. You can also offer a VIP package whereby you collapse more time and instead of one-hour sessions over six weeks, you could offer a crash course in one day and charge more at 5.000. Again, you are saving time and a lot of effort for the client by giving them all the information in one swoop, so charging more is totally acceptable.

You are your own boss, so you get to call the shots!

Check out my amazing money mindset course and get yourself a juicy 50 % discount with the coupon code "BOOK"! (*See also Chapter 5.2 for more on the money mindset.*)

https://www.christinemeansbusiness.com/mmjj

5 Steps to Get You to $5,000 a Month with Amanda Daley

Okay, let's talk some more about money. You're a BUSINESS after all. Here's the thing though: Money is connected to ALL THE THINGS in this book. Just check out the list below. It's about mindset, your business model, your ideal client. And that's beautiful. It's part of it ALL. And don't worry, I'm a straight-talking gal, I won't keep numbers from you.

1. **Mindset.** Feeling like a fraud is a mindset, it's not you. It's a beginner thing…okay, fine, it will creep up on you over and over no matter how long you are in the business. Realize everybody feels like this. And it's okay. We can make ourselves too special in a negative sense – EVERYBODY deals with feeling like a fraud. Who you surround yourself with is THE KEY. Check out my amazing money mindset course and bag 50% off with the coupon code "BOOK"! https://www.christinemeansbusiness.com/mmjj

2. **Having the right business model**. Important: The right one for YOU. You don't have to be a millionaire. Many business models focus on that. But if that's not what you want, then it's not for you. Get out a calculator and work out how many clients you need to make what you want.

Make purposeful packages the foundation of your business.

Find the sweet spot between single sessions and packages. Once you've got your business plan you can start low ($500 per package), if you're not feeling confident for example, but at some point, you can raise your prices. Doing one-on-one sessions will give you the initial confidence to make packages later (or, in my opinion, as soon as possible).

3. **Eyeballs.** Who is your ideal client? By identifying your ideal client you can make marketing magnetic. Identify the one ideal client (*See Chapter 1.2*). Ask yourself every day how you want to be seen and how you can attract that one ideal client and get them to buy. People think if they only talk to one person they won't get clients or that they will not help other people. Not true!

Marketing should feel like having a coffee together.

4. **Ask for the dance.** How do we get from your client's eyeballs to asking for a dance? That's the bridge to getting on the sales call. **Your job is to get people on the phone.** Put a call to action in your socials, BUT we are in the age of DMs for reaching out and creating authentic relationships (only when invited! Don't be a slimy creep sliding into people's DMs pretending to want to "just help." We all see through that). When someone reaches out to you start a genuine conversation, we do have to go the extra step.

If you want to be in business, you have to market.

If you just want to help people, give them content and ask how you can help. No need to get all competitive, it's all about collaboration. Not everyone is meant for you. Find those who are.

You don't want everyone. You don't need everyone.

5. **Soulful sales and systems**. Is the potential client ready to transform? Am I the coach for them? That is the only energy you want in a sales / discovery call. A sales call should be 100% about the client. Allow your client to go high in your dreams. Take them on that journey. And then bring them back down to earth and be honest what that pain is doing. By doing that, you can see if they're ready to transform. The only other thing you need to know then, is if it's the right time. If a client isn't ready, why would you want to take that on? It's going to take you back to step 1: feeling like a fraud.

Remember not to shame anyone into anything. A useful and helpful question can be: why are you reaching out now? You're a lighthouse, remember?

How to Sell on Black Friday so it Puts Money IN your Wallet

Is discounting worth it?

Black Friday is an excellent time for you to sell your wares as an online marketer.

Warning: DO NOT discount your one-on-one sessions! Here's why:

Discounting stuff rarely makes you or your client happy (it's a bit different if you're selling physical products). You really need to understand the psychology behind a discount: discounting is taking value OFF your stuff. So, I really don't support shaving off your price tag when it is connected to your services. What a lot of people do is discount their one-on-one and it's going to psychologically make you sell with resentment. We know our worth, and when people buy at a discounted price there's a certain tint to it. It just makes you look less serious and takes away from your qualifications. With a one-on-one, your time is involved. And people have a different vibe going in when they know there's a discount.

So, what should you do instead?

Deal not discount.

Instead of offering a discount to your precious services, you can offer a deal. Here's how: Pull an extra from your resources and use that as an add-on. *Tadaaaa.*

Even if all you do is one-on-one sessions, you can pull something from your one-on-one – a resource, a video series, a guide, recipes, meal plans – something you can sell for a Black Friday promo. Even if you just sell it for $17 or whatever, that will give you a little income and experience launching over a short time period. PLUS, people are going to see how awesome you are! It's also a great way to warm up people on your mailing list. It's a small first transaction potential clients can engage with to see if they want more. I always insist on creating forever content, so if you have a blog or podcast, for example, you can turn it into an awesome book (like this one)!

> ### TOOLBOX
>
> Beacon.by
> Use beacon.by software to convert your blog posts into pdfs to sell.
> The software copies the url from your blog and converts into a pdf.

If you're wondering whether people will buy if it's already free on your website: the answer is YES. People will buy to get a bundle. Otherwise, they would have to go looking and pull everything together themselves. They're paying for the convenience and time saved.

Stuff you can put together to form awesome bundles.

- Record a couple of meditations. Make a digital product.
- Make a video lesson bundle from your YouTube content. Nothing is as personal as videos.
- Create a special mini product: a 21-day coaching programme or bootcamp. Offer limited amounts.
- Offer a license to programmes they can customize with their brand.

It's all about getting your foot in the door with potential clients.

Think it's cheating to repurpose content? Well, I'm all for cheating in this respect!

You can pre-sell something you don't have yet.

You can pre-sell a paid workshop you'll do in December, for example. A couple weeks before, you can send out a tease via email: this thing is going on promotion on Black Friday. Let people know via socials, etc. Don't take too long for the promotion, start on the Monday for Friday. (People are always already flooded with spam.) Send out your email sequence. Most people prefer to buy through email vs social media. Many people will buy on the last day. People need to see and get reminders. When you're promoting you will get unsubscribes, DO NOT WORRY ABOUT IT.

Now, if you're thinking, but I want it to discount my one-on-one, you can do that too without shaving money off your price tag. Instead of taking value away, give more value. This way, you don't discredit what you have but you add something. You can add an extra session, create something new – a cheat sheet, customized meditation, a recipe book, a food and sleep diary. Add 3-5 easy bonuses. You give extra and don't discount yourself!

Insider tip: I've never been happy working with the people who are attracted by discounts.

Biz Bomb

What to do When a Client Can't Afford You

I'm coming at you with an amazing tip in this chapter. I call it **The Back Pocket Offer**. This is a neat offer to have on hand when you need a quick cash injection or when you have someone on the initial call who wants to work with you, but you can tell that your signature program is **genuinely too expensive** for them, and they're not interested in a DIY course either.

This is when you whip out that Back Pocket Offer. This offer can be a hybrid of your highest and lowest offer, or a stand-alone that is in the mid-range price point.

Important: Don't advertise your Back Pocket Offer! It's something you whip out when it feels right on a sales call.

BUT: I always want you to go high enough price wise that you don't need a ridiculous number of sales every month to make a good income. I'm all about that good work-life balance: more life, less work!

My offers.

- **My tiny offer:** changes all the time but check out my website and you will see the current one.
- **My course:** It covers the main five pillars of my Impact with Integrity Method and then some, depending on whether I add Live Q&A, sells between $999-$1,997 (depending on when you sign up and what I add as extras).

- **Private Coaching**: These services are never less than $5,000. That includes private calls with me. And that means you get so much more support and bespoke strategy and all my resource knowledge when you work with me privately.

- **Back Pocket Offer** (or hybrid offer): This offer is in the mid-range (around $3,000 but don't quote me on that). Clients get my course plus some calls with me. The philosophy of this offer is that a client can implement everything on their own through the course, but they do have the support of the one-on-one as well. That helps them stay accountable and to implement strategies. I find it works really well but it always depends on the client, of course.

My Back Pocket Offer is not a lot of work for me, but it gives my clients a lot of bang for their buck.

If you don't have masterclasses or a course, you could see how you can adapt your offer to make it a little bit less work for you and a bit more for your client – that way, less of your time is involved. Have a look at what you have – any material that's already done – and then price it at a sweet spot. If you don't have a course yet, but you want to do one in the future, think about what that price point will be, and that might also help you to find that sweet spot for your Back Pocket Offer. And then, just try it next time you're on a call and you genuinely notice that the person cannot afford your signature service.

Check out all my offers and how I market them on https://www. christinemeansbusiness.com

3. Marketing

Section 3

MARKETING

My philosophy for marketing is that when you're a business it's all about YOU. I've got a very business owner-centered approach because if we are genuine about ourselves, represent ourselves the way that we are, then we're going to attract the right clients. It's not about assuming what someone else likes (*see Chapter 1.1*). It's about starting with yourself.

For me, a good framework is this: **For me, for you, for us**. It always starts with **me**. The extension of that is for **you** and then for **us**, the community. Most importantly, marketing has to be genuine, it has to be authentic, do not promise things that are not real. Do not only promise results from your best-case scenario – be honest with people.

I don't believe in shaming in marketing, making someone feel horrible to get them to buy. It's about showing them, and possibly making them aware of, what they need.

You're there for them when they're ready.

How I lost my Insta.

In October 2020, I lost my complete Insta with 12,000 followers due to the robots that were policing social media during the US election. It was not possible to get it back. I had to start again and, within my first month and with less than 400 followers, I got my first paying client through my new Insta. I don't think I ever got a paying client so quickly out of my 12,000 strong following on my old Insta account. And it's all because I changed my strategy to one that is very genuine, honest, where I only speak if I have something to say.

So remember, more followers does not equal more money. Creating engagement and a community is more important than high follower numbers.

My new Insta is now an extension of me. Check it out: @bychristine_hansen. That's what marketing is all about.

Showing who you are.

SEO

What is SEO & How to Use it to Grow Your Business with Stephanie Fiteni

Okay, first things first: what on earth is SEO and why do you need to know about it?

Stephanie: *"SEO stands for Search Engine Optimization and is basically little tweaks to websites and social media to optimize them for keywords so Google can see what you're about. Optimizing means putting keywords in the right place. **The aim of every website and blog post is to rank as high as possible."***

SEO makes you money by saving you time.

The funnel.

In order to build your business, keeping in touch with people via your email list is important. So, a funnel simply means a tool on your website that grows your email list. For example: Use a blog post to attract to your website and then offer something on your funnel page to entice people to join your email list. That's a funnel. It can also be a freebie or PDF people get if they join your list. That way you also know what they're interested in. (*For the lowdown on building your funnel, go to Chapter 3.2*) To see how my funnel works go to *https://www.christinemeansbusiness.com/free-class/* and see it in action.

Using keywords.

Let's say you're a health coach and you specialize in curing migraines. Somebody looking for help with their migraine might google "best migraine medication." However, health coaches will probably not use medication; they might use other techniques, such as meditation. So, as a health coach, what you need to do is to catch the traffic that is looking for the most basic, fastest solution to a problem, and then educate people **to buy into what you're selling**. In the above case, you could educate why pills may not be best solution, for example.

An example for a great keyword from my business, *Sleep Like A Boss*, would be "sleeping pills," because people are looking for that even though I don't sell it!

How many keywords do you need?

Ideally, one keyword for each piece of content. If you're producing one piece of content a week for a year, you'll need 52 keywords. It helps to have 3 categories to collect keywords in. Decide what three topics you want to optimize your website for. Then collect all of your keywords in these three categories.

Within those keyword categories you don't want to have too much competition or you won't have a chance to surface; however, you don't want to be irrelevant either or nobody will be looking for you. So, the sweet spot is this: find a group of high-ranking keywords (that are used a lot), i.e., that have a lot of competition, and use low-ranking keywords within that group that don't have a lot of competition. So, your category cluster is a high-ranking keyword, and the keywords you collect within that cluster should be low-ranking. Imagine a little army of low-ranking keywords pushing the high-ranking keyword (used by your competitors) to the front of peoples' searches.

Now, where to put those pesky keywords? You need a keyword in your title. In the first paragraph. Put it into subtitles, but use it only in the first subtitle, and then use synonyms in subsequent subtitles. Still with me? Take an example: your keyword is 'medication' in the first subtitle, in the second, use "pills," or "drugs," etc.

Does competition matter with SEO?

If competition is high and loads of other websites rank higher than yours, chances are people are already spending money on SEO, so it's unlikely you can get in on that fast. BUT Stephanie has an amazing tip: begin with finding out a number of keywords for yourself that are low competition. It's that simple !

119

TOOLBOX:

UberSuggest: free but slow.

SEO PowerSuite: good for beginners.

Mangools: a little toolkit to help you with various SEO tasks.

You want three things from tools: more suggestions, competition, price per click. Choose keywords that have a high price per click.

Local SEO (if you have a practice): being local makes it easier. Get a Google Business page with a location on maps, keywords, services, opening hours. Google will then suggest you more likely.

Remember: It pays to keep updated on SEO matters. Things change so much.

Okay, SEO and where else to put it? Stephanie's top tips.

- Podcast show notes: have a transcript with the complete podcast but also a summary. Turn the transcription into a blogpost. Make sure people stay on the page. Start with a story then add information.
- Blog tags (usually easy to find when creating a new post): it helps to have 1 or 2. The best place to source them is

Google. Search for "can't sleep" for example and at the very bottom of the page you'll see related searches. Those are topics that Google has connected to a particular keyword. It's always good to check your competition using keyword tools once you've decided on a keyword.

- YouTube: put your keyword in the very beginning. You have to make sure you use the right title right away because Google doesn't change it in their database even if you make changes later. Create your title like this: **Title = keyword + subtitle.** Leave quite a long description with your keywords. Try not to make it a direct transcript of the video. Add your videos to playlists, your own and other people's.

Christine's top tip: For SEO purposes, is it better to write a new blog post, edit an old one, or delete the old completely? The answer is that it all depends on how much of the content you want to change. If you want to change about 20% of your old post, Google sees this as positive. But if you change 60%, Google will see it as a new post. If you have an old post that's not connected to others, it's better to delete.

Social social social.

Social media platforms are some of the highest-ranking websites on the planet (currently, Google and YouTube are neck and neck for number 1, followed by Facebook – all depending on who you ask, of course). So, if you get links back from these sites, they're going to count big time, says Stephanie. Search engines also read how much engagement you get on social media. When you're linking something to a page or website, if you use a particular keyword you used on that page in the text than Google will understand more. Pay particular attention to YouTube, Pinterest, and LinkedIn as they are more like a search engine than Twitter or Instagram for example, even though Instagram is starting to change that and be more focused with their search bar through hashtags.

SEO is like other people talking about you.

TOOLBOX

Confused by Google Analytics? Here's another solution.

Cyfe.com

Integrates with Google Analytics and Facebook, Pinterest, Instagram, YouTube, etc. It will tell you what your most popular posts are, where you get traffic from. Much more cleaned up than Google Analytics. It's free for up to 5 platforms to analyse.

> **NELIO**
>
> Once you've written a blog post, it allows you to autofill your social media. (except Insta)
>
> Similar: **Missinglettr.**

Email

How to Write a Super Selling Email with Travis Baird

Emails are really amazing tools to get clients. Think they're old-fashioned? Think again! Travis Beard shows us the amazingness of your email list.

The welcome sequence.

The first set of emails a new subscriber gets when they join your email list is called the welcome sequence. It takes the moment when a new subscriber is at their most enthusiastic about you and gives you the chance to control that journey.

The concept for any email is the same as for cold pitching: The focus must lie on what the receiving person **needs** and how you can help them. This email bridges the gap between: "I just found out about you" to "OMG I really want to work with you."

Important: Make sure that every new subscriber only gets your welcome sequence when they start. Every other email you send should not go to those who are still getting the welcome sequence!

Christine's hot take: The content for new subscribers should be a bit softer than your regular mailing list content.

Your welcome email should be totally unique. Follow Travis' awesome guidelines here:

The first thing you need is to start with a goal. The goal? Getting people on a sales call or purchasing something for example.

With your goal in mind, each email in your welcome sequence will take people from freebie or sign up to the next step – **one step across the bridge to where you want them to go**.

How do you take them across that bridge? One great way is through stories (remember my awesome chapter on storytelling? If not, check it out again in Section 2.)

One email, one goal.

Telling one story, sharing one lesson, giving one resource, getting on a call, selling one thing. Focus on just that one thing. So, don't have your Insta or Facebook at the bottom of the email if that email is not about it. It's distracting. A round up at the end is fine. **Do everything intentionally and with awareness**. Know why you are putting what kind of content in your email. If you have a lot to tell, awesome, send a lot of different emails!

Travis' 3 steps to email success.

1. Show that you can be trusted.
Tell your potential client: It's okay that you're here and this is why. You don't have to be stuck in this place. It's not your fault. I understand where you're at.
2. Go into teaching.
Share your core values.
3. From there, go into selling. What do you want them to do? Get on a discovery call? Tell them: This is how I help people.
You need to come from a place of empathy, of understanding, of caring.
Say: Here, this is the next step and we can do this together.
Validate their concerns.

The nitty gritty on emails.

Consistency is the key for regular newsletters. I would suggest sending one every 2 weeks or consider how your email list is segmented. Ask yourself for each email: *does everybody need to get this email?* If someone just bought something they will not want an email about that product, and it will even feel like you're not paying attention to them.

When writing an email ask yourself: will readers be able to figure out why it's important to them? I see so many emails that are just about "me." People don't want news from you unless it will benefit them. Analyze other people's emails, more often than not they're too complex.

The idea of practicing mindfulness is simple but not easy. This also applies to writing emails.

Write emails with intent.

Top tip: Have a place to capture ideas (a file, etc.) where you collect ideas that you can turn into amazing emails.

Christine's hot take: I've taken courses, done the training but, in the end, I'm comfortable with spending a lot of money on copywriters. (I just spent $20.000 on a retainer for a copy writer).

If you can afford to, it's money well spent. They just know what they're doing.

If there's one step you want to take right now, go to my website and sign up to my email list to see my sequence in action! AND you'll also get my awesome workbook all about funnels.

www.christinemeansbusiness/AAF.

Email Marketing: How to Write a Kickass Subject Line

Why you still need an email list.

You need to get people off social onto email. It's a reliable way to communicate with people. All of your launches should be scaled to the size of your list. It's about people being engaged. Just because you have a lot of people following doesn't mean you're making money.

Remember: It's a fine balance, people will sign up to your list because you're bribing them. Everyone is annoyed by emails. Right!?

In order for people to sign up, you need to give them something.

Three kinds of people will sign up to your email.

a. The person who is genuinely interested in you. Who enjoys the way you are and who is playing with the idea of hiring your services.

b. The tire kicker. The sceptic but it's free, so why not.

c. The people simply wanting free stuff. The percentage of these people who sign up is low.

Top tip: Every 3 months I purge my list: whoever doesn't engage, has to go, even if they're subscribed. Even if growth is slow, the people who remain are the ones I want to work with.

Example:

I organized the Women's Divine Sleep Summit – an interview series with experts related to the field. It was free for a certain time, people signed up via email. Then, I sold the content at the end. People couldn't consume everything in the time it was free. But they could buy what they had missed at the end. This grew my email list loads, but six months later my list was pretty much the same as before. Here's the thing: the people who signed up? They were not that serious because it was free. And they didn't buy the recording and extras for $47. I did a survey on why it didn't sell, and people said it was too expensive. Now, remember,

I'm a high-end business. As you can imagine, 90% of my clients were not even on that new part of my email list. (*How I get my clients? See Chapters 3.3 and 3.4*)

So be clear on who you want to be and who you want to attract. Then you have to figure out what your audience is interested in. And it is ALWAYS worth signing people up to a list – even if only to figure out what they want!

Build your email from the beginning. When you sell mid to low ticket, an email list is the way to grow.

Me? My tickets to work with me privately are a minimum of $5,000. What can I say? I'm a luxury product. I don't hard sell via email, not at the moment anyway. Still, I **love** the people on my list, and I get interesting feedback from them.

Your email list has return customers. That doesn't work on social media. You need to keep them interested. Keep them safe in your email list.

Email list providers.

Do. No. Use. Gmail. It's not professional and it will get you into trouble as you legally need an email software provider to communicate with groups of people for your business.

I also don't recommend Mailchimp – they penalize you on the number of people you have on your list and are really difficult to use actually and get really expensive when you grow.

I do recommend MailerLite and Flodesk. They are both affordable, easy to use, and get the job done. They can also handle complex funnels. Check out my referral links here and get yourself a deal:

https://www.christinemeansbusiness.com/Mailerlite

http://www.christinemeansbusiness.com/flodesk

Other good providers: Drip. Constant Contact. GetResponse. ConvertKit. Active Campaign.

All providers work pretty much the same way, it's a drag and drop kind of thing.

Side note: what to include depends on what you're selling. If it's products, you need images, gifs, etc. What converts best in the beginning (not to spam), is to have just your text (plus the unsubscribe button), your address (so that your inbox sees you are a legit business and doesn't banish you into the promo folder), and no links. If people want to reply, say just reply to this email. I don't even use colours sometimes. Can you imagine? Mostly black text, some pink. No images. Looks more serious and businessy.

Once you have people start opening your emails, you can add images etc. because then you won't be going into spam. Saves time too!

The first question.

In your first email, ask your recipients to reply to the email with something quick. E.g., out of ten where would you rate your fatigue? If people reply, your future email won't go into their spam. Neat, right? Also, it's good market research. You can see what words their using, what problems they have.

For example, ask: What are your sleep struggles? I reply (yes, it's actually me replying, not my assistant), and I say if they want more info to schedule a call. And ideally, that'll be a future client. Boom.

The subject line.

Your subject line will make or break your open rate. The industry standard for health and wellness is about 20 % open rate.

Here's a bad subject line: "October newsletter." For one, it's boring. Two, it gives away the clinch of the email in the subject line, and that is always a bad idea. You want people to be intrigued. Make your subject line personal. Do NOT do clickbait! (See glossary for definition.)

Top tip: If you have Gmail, go into your promotions folder and see what works and what doesn't.

TOOLBOX

talkingshrimp.com
Check out Laura Belgray's headlines. They are simply amazing. I actually have a folder with her newsletter and get inspired by her subject lines!
Obviously, don't steal!

Email Marketing: the legal stuff

The legal stuff.

Okay, let's get down to the boring stuff. It may be tedious, but this stuff is so important.

Being professional is doing things right.

Now, legal requirements vary per country, so you need to check your individual requirements. BUT you always need to get people's permission. This is so important. You can't just use people's emails for something other than what they signed up for. Imagine you're at a networking event and you exchange business cards with people. You're not allowed to take those emails and put them into your list. Even when organising giveaways or wins – if you collect people's emails, you need a disclaimer that you will email them. The same is true for sales calls: people who gave you their email to get a reminder of the call DID NOT accept to be on your mailing list. Unless you inform them when they sign up and they accept.

Opting in.

There are two ways people can opt-in to your mailing list: single or double.

The Single: a one-step process that requires the person to enter their email once in a sign-up box on a website. There is no confirmation, and they are immediately subscribed.

The Double: a two-step process. Step one is to enter their email into a sign-up box on a website. Step two is receiving a confirmation email in which they must click to confirm subscription before being added to your list.

If you have the double opt-in, people are more likely to engage later. After all, they twice decided to opt-in. Make sure there is a message to check their spam for the second email.

All of these emails need to be in your voice. People are giving away something personal, you need to tell them what's going to happen: *You'll get this email and there's the thing, check your spam,* etc. It builds trust. The second email: customize it, brand it. So people see it's you behind your business and not just a robot. Put the name of the thing in your subject line plus "download" whatever the freebie is. This is not the time to sell. Don't pitch in this email.

GDPR.

The EU made it illegal to collect data in certain ways. You can't ever give info to a third party. Another thing you really need on your website: a privacy policy and GDPR section. Personally, I invested in a template by a lawyer.

Every step you add is going to put people off.
So make it fun.

TOOLBOX

Podcast: Being Boss: Mindset, Habits, Tactics, and Lifestyle for Creative Entrepreneurs

Your six-step email nurture sequence

Your email nurture sequence or email funnel is a sequence of emails to new subscribers to build trust, get to know you and your method, and how you can help them. It is important not to pitch too quickly. People need time to warm up.

Disclaimer: My welcome sequence changes all the time. That's because I change. The example below is a healthy staple though that has shown to be successful with most people when the writing is true to its author's voice.

Follow my 6-step email sequence to get started.

1. Email 1: setting the stage and delivering your free offer. Delivering your offer is non-negotiable. You can either have that as a re-direct from where they signed up with their email and then you also send them your welcome email. Or you have a thank you for subscribing text pop

up and a note to check their email where they will find your welcome email with the freebie. (I recommend the latter.)

Mention what your next email will be called and let them know when they might get it to be on the lookout. You need to have a goal in mind and then reverse engineer it for your email sequence.

You can have several funnels. If you have products, DIY templates, supplements, you can have different op-ins on your website that lead to different emails. But your personality should be the same for all.

2. Email 2: (1 hour, 1 day, 2 days later) tell them your compelling story. Here's the cold, hard truth: people don't really care about your story. But what they do care about is how your story **can help them**. Refer back to your audience: *Is this familiar? Can you relate?* They are the star of the show. End the email at the most dramatic climax of your story. Sprinkle testimonials into your story. *This helped my client*, etc. Add: *Reply to this email if you have a question.* (Also, this gives you free research on people's problems!)

    BUT don't do too many emails. Don't start annoying people.

AND give people value, but don't worry about re-inventing the wheel. Link to an old blog post of yours.

3. Email 3: tell how you (or how you helped your client) solve the problem (pick up on your story). *This is how I can solve yours.*

4. Email 4: aggravate the problem and surprise them.

First, make them feel that this is a problem. E.g., Tired all the time. Speak to pain points. Try to think of issues in relation to one bigger problem.

Second, empower them that they have power to change their situation. That's the surprise. You can change your issue. **This is in your control**. And tell them it's not their fault.

When you don't have your own story use your client's story. For the surprise: *what she didn't know...*

People connect to stories. Create a narrative.

5. Email 5: testimonial (you need permission to use a person's image*). So and so was able to get_____ solved by using your method. If you don't have client yet, use yourself, your friend, family. Throughout, give, ,give, give*: Oh, by the way here's one of my most popular blog posts. Or give them a free training. In email 5 you can also

do a call to action: start asking for something: *why don't you book a call if you have questions.* Don't tell them about your paying programme yet. Do a P.S. *check out my Insta* (= microconversions).

You want people to know you before you pitch them something.

6. Email 6: full pitch. Explain your method and how it has helped you or your clients. Outline your step-by-step process. *Click here if this is for you.* Or link to a free sales call. You can tell people you only work with a certain number of clients at a time (for me it's 5). Even if it's not true, it will help those still on the fence. *I'm opening up my schedule for a certain amount of people* triggers FOMO. Don't worry if the person still doesn't book. That's why you're sending weekly emails. To get people closer to booking. Follow up with people who have booked a sales call but not bought yet. Don't forget that you are there to serve and make their lives better: but ultimately you are a business, and they know that and know you will sell to them. And that's okay!

Top tip: Don't be scared to use pictures (only not in the first email).

In the beginning, you just give.

TOOLBOX

Use Dubb to Personalize Your Lead Emails

http://www.christinemeansbusiness.com/dubb

Dubb is a software that allows you to record a
little video on your desktop or on their chrome
extension. It's super easy to embed into email. You can
personalize and customize the video. You can have a
call-to-action button and a description. It helps you
deliver that personal touch.

A video is so much more personal than a text. Use
it for leads or to thank someone for enrolling in a
course. Or even use it for pitching to media!

Why Your Lead Magnet Isn't Converting

The lead magnet.

The lead magnet is also called a freebie, free gift, free offer, or
opt-in. It can be a link or a button on your website. The purpose
of a lead magnet is to get people onto your email list. You have to

bribe and entice people to join. That's just how it is. If you say: *subscribe to my newsletter!* People are going to be like *why?*

You could be giving away a cheat sheet, a check list, eBook, web series, video; something for free and of value. That way, you can get to know and nurture people, and they become future clients. Plus, you're giving them something valuable – so don't feel bad about it!

I would actually encourage you to go the extra mile and add an extra bonus. Like an audio file going into depth on the topics of your cheat sheet for example, or a meditation that suits the topic, or a video tutorial on how to use the resource they just received.

BUT you need to get permission and be clear and transparent that you're asking people to join your marketing list. They need to say **yes** to that. Otherwise, it's illegal (don't worry, I have a section on all the legal stuff below).

Examples of a lead magnet.

- check list
- report
- eBook (used to be more popular)
- mini class

- training over a few days
- Plus Bonuses if you truly want to make an impact

How to get those precious emails.

How do you get those email addresses? There are a few options. You can have a landing page; a single page that tells people why you should subscribe. The difference to a website is that on a landing page there is nothing to distract you, no menu, no options. It just contains the information about the mailing list. It focuses on selling visitors the idea that they need this and the currency they pay with is their email address.

Converting from email to a sale.

How do you get people from your email list and lead them to a sale? Or to a free sales call or offer? First, you need the conversion: Check how many people see your landing page and how many sign up. If a lot of people see it but not a lot sign up then something is wrong. Those who give their email, how many of those are purchasing something?

Your lead magnet may be too much of a chore to consume. Back in the day, eBooks were great. But people don't have that attention span anymore. If people don't get to the end of your freebie, it won't convert. What you want is people to get a result from your lead magnet.

You need instant gratification.

Check out my own lead magnet, which is the ultimate check list for your online business: *www.christinemeansbusiness/ultimate-checklist (by the time this goes into print it will not be publicly available any more but only for you guys who read this!)*

Give them a hot tip or tell them something they didn't know. For example, for my sleep business, I can use this: *Here are 5 sleep choices you didn't know about.*

If you want to do a guide, call it a quick guide. A quick video. Quick review. *The 5 best supplements for your thyroid.*

If it's ten minutes, it's too long. 5 minutes is perfect. People love the numbers 3 and 5. Or the number 1 thing. *The One Thing That'll Make You Sleep Better.* Make it juicy.

Know your audience.

Cater for where you audience is at; are they beginners or more advanced? Your juicy piece of info needs to fit with what they know. If you give an advanced health coach a beginner's tip, they're not going to find it interesting.

Make sure you know your niche. (*See Chapter 1.2 for all about niching.*)

Are you pitching your lead magnet often enough? You need to tell people about your lead magnet more than once. Whenever you post: *Did you know I have a free* … Every time you're showing up on social media.

BUT don't just tell people about your lead magnet, you need to provide valuable content on socials and then the lead magnet is an extra. People are very sensitive to being marketed to especially on social media as it is **not** meant to be a marketing platform! It is meant to be social!

I regularly pitch on my blog with a popup. So, I link to my blog from socials, so you've already got content and then I'm a bit in your face with the pop up.

Have a lead magnet in your email signature.

If you want to get into podcasts, articles, on guest posts, people will usually allow you to offer your free gift to the audience or readers of their post.

Super pro tip: When on a podcast you can design a lead magnet for the audience you're talking to.

You can create links through a redirect. I use a plugin called 301redirect, where I can create links and then redirect it to some other page.

People are **so flattered** if you address them directly. I.e., when I was on Entrepreneur on Fire my link ended with /fire (something a lot of people do on that podcast and John Lee Dumas encourages) and the lead page started with "Hey Firestarter," which is what he calls his audience.

Multiple lead magnets?

If you are new, just make one. Make it super specific to your audience. In the future, you can make more. Especially if you work with a team later on.

Connect to your business.

Make sure your lead magnet is not disconnected from your business. It needs to be something that leads directly from what your audience is looking for. Obvious connection: where do they need to go first when they come into contact with your business?

Make sure your lead magnet conveys what kind of service you have (e.g., simple or complicated).

Story time: I had a bedtime routine checklist for Sleep Like A Boss, but it's not really what I do. So then, my lead magnet was a free training, and it actually showed people what they don't know. So, they want to hire us to find out even more.

One big lead magnet I see all the time is quizzes. Quizzes convert well to step one (signing up), but step two (leading to sales) is not happening. I'm not a fan because of that. People take quizzes when they're bored, it doesn't mean they're interested.

Top tip: When you create a lead magnet make sure it's something that you want to keep for a long time. It will take you a while to figure the right one out. Your lead magnet will last for a long time. So it's important that you choose something you can stick with for a long time, especially if you promoted a specific url on a podcast where people can listen to your episode even 10 years later.

Insider tip: In an interview if someone asks you what your lead magnet is, I would refrain from being too specific. Say something like it's a tool to help with xxx and you can find it on my website.

Does your landing page suck?

You can get them out of the box, so no excuse. There should be no unnecessary stuff, it should be all about that free gift. You want a huge headline, a subtitle, and then the sign up. Make sure everything is above the fold (no scrolling necessary). You can add a video, testimonials, media credibility afterwards. Make sure it's easy to read, choose a big font, and **check it's mobile friendly**!!!

Some people do like to get more information, so for them you include the stuff at the bottom (testimonials, videos, bio). For impulsive people, they just need the info above the fold. Make sure you have an option to sign up at the beginning AND at end of the page.

If it's not working, don't change everything at once. Change one thing at a time. Because if your lead magnet isn't working and you change everything, and you get results, you won't know what it was that didn't work. Duh.

Believe it or not, the colour of your sign-up button is important. Don't make it too aggressive, too red. The font is important too. Do some research on this. There are plenty of studies and blog posts online. Give it time and run it for one to two weeks before you judge results.

Don't ask for too much info. No phone number. I even find a name is too much sometimes. I just ask for their email address most of the time. I know you can customize your email newsletter to include the name people signed up with, so it's *Hi Christine* or whatever. But sometimes people don't use their full name, just their initials, or something else completely. So, I wouldn't do it. You don't know who filled it in.

For some that personalisation option might work well though. At the end of the day, you need to figure out what works for you!

Legal stuff

Right. Got to talk about some boring stuff. You're a business, it's all part of being professional. So, reward yourself with your favourite cookies, cocktail, or curry and **Get. It. Done.**

What you need: a privacy policy and GDPR consent form. (*I have a whole bit on this at the beginning of this section.*)

Facebook, for example, checks whether you have a privacy policy and GDPR if you're doing ads. You need a link to list your privacy policy on your website. Regulations are different in the EU vs the US and across the globe, so check the guidelines. Some email providers do this for you. There might be an extra GDPR box to click. Yes, it's another step but that might not be bad because it means the people signing up are extra committed.

1 step opt-in: a field right on your landing page or a box that opens where you type details. Statistically, 2 steps are better leads in the end because people are more committed. In Canada for example it's the law that they have to confirm the subscription.

I have a large number of subscribers who have not confirmed, and I just get rid of them. If they can't be bothered to click that second link, then they will probably never become a client!

Five reasons your lead magnet sucks.

1. Too difficult, too long
2. Nobody knows about it
3. Has nothing to do with what you serve or sell
4. Landing page is just bad
5. Content is not good enough

TOOLBOX

I often like to discuss ideas with a biz buddy through voice messages and my favorite app for that is
Voxer App
Pro version: transcription button.
I also use it as extra support for my clients.

The Funnel: the flirt, the date, and the wedding

First up, a warning: Beware of the funnel-building courses, blueprints, etc. that say you will make millions from this funnel. "Just set it and forget it." Sorry, babe, that is just not how it works. Also, beware of too complex software. Often, the complexity will just lead to overwhelm. You might feel you've been duped, you will be frustrated – not a good thing to be when building your business!

What is it?

I liked to say a funnel is like a dating process. It should be a natural money-making process. If you think about your funnel like dating (yes, with people!) it'll give you such a different vibe. Don't think: leads, prospects, customers, dollars. Think: relationships.

Steps of a funnel.

1. **Flirting.** Be on the radar of your soulmate clients. Always remember my lighthouse metaphor – you are what you are, your personality is what it is, and you stand for something, and you SHOULD NOT BUDGE unless you want to.

Ways to flirt: Facebook ad campaign that doesn't ask for anything from your audience, but it introduces you to them. Make a video that really shows who you are, maybe even on an issue that is close to your heart but you know divides people.

A second way to flirt is through organic content, so through social media (short-term content) and Google, blog posts, Pinterest (long-term content). (*For all things content, check out Chapter 3.3 and 3.4.*)

A third way to flirt is through PR. That is, being in online magazines, journals, on TV, radio.

People should love you for who you are. It's the same in business.

2. **The date.** A small commitment. This is about asking potentially interested people to go on a date with you. Now, this doesn't mean marriage, but it means a small commitment. So, in the funnel world this means people giving you their email address or a small fee in exchange for something. This something is called opt-ins or freebies or free gifts (i.e., checklist, ebook, audio recording, etc.) or a tiny offer. The date itself is the lead page. The page where you ask for a small commitment.

3. **The wedding.** The higher sale. That might be a sales page or an email workflow that asks to buy a product

or schedule a call to work with you. And don't be shy about this – people know you're a business, they know you sell things.

The lead page.

Characteristics of a lead page:

- No distractions. Nothing to entice people to click away (i.e., a menu)
- Have your button above the fold. Make it clear and simple.
- Talk about the benefits, benefits, benefits of why they should give you their email.
- The copy should make people aware of their struggle, intensify that struggle, and then offer a solution and benefits (i.e., how it will change their life).

Head over to my website and see my own lead page in action! www.christinemeansbusiness/AAF In fact, my lead page will get you an awesome workbook all about funnels, so what are you waiting for?

Now, you're all set for your email sequence to start. Read on in the next section to find out all about the best way to sell via email.

Think this is all too complex and starting to feel overwhelmed?

I have something for you.

The kiss.

1 page, 1 email, done.

You don't even need a website, just a landing page (you can get one through your email software provider). You send one email – the delivery email – and you're done.

I'm telling you, it works.

Long-term Content

Long-term content creation

Content gets you clients for free, organically. You can get clients through ads, but that can be a risky business if you don't know what you're doing, and it is quite complex. It's a whole book on itself that would probably need to be updated every six months minimum. Ads also don't always get the right type of client. If you want to work with your dream, soulmate clients there's nothing as powerful as organic content. Ultimately, it'll help you get greater reach (*see Chapter 3.3 on blogging*).

Types of content.

You need a good mix of long-term content and short-term content. **Long-term content** is what is searchable. Someone is actively searching for that content. The searcher expects to find answers to their question. Where do people search? Search engines Google, YouTube, and Pinterest. Long-term content is there to educate. Share your wisdom and expertise.

Short-term content is social media. People don't go onto socials to learn, they want to have fun, be inspired, etc. Social content: we are what we sell. We stand for your values.

Your frequency.

As much as you can handle. There are 52ish weeks in a year. If you want to put out weekly posts, 52 per year is definitely doable. Split into two, publish biweekly that's 26 pieces. You can even split it further, publish once a month, so then you're doing 12 pieces a year. The more you publish, the higher your chances that you will rank and be found. Google wants to be wined and dined (no one-night stands here); give it good content. It'll take around six months to convert.

My secret weapon for all of this is batching. Think of it as meal-prepping for content. I choose one week where I prepare content for the next two to three months. My main blog posts go out every two weeks. These pieces of content can be solo pieces or interviews. Because I choose a week to do this, I can choose to create content when I feel like it (it's so much better when I'm in a good mood). So, I would sit down for an hour and record six videos of 4-6 minutes approximately. That is my content for 12 weeks done, or I batch my interviews during one month to cover the next four. Check out my blogs:

https://www.christinemeansbusiness.com/blog

Your pillars.

Do a little business audit and decide what your main values are in your business.

So, for Christine Means Business my main strategic pillars are: branding and niching, pricing and packaging, email and tech, content creation and global outreach. Then, my personal pillars are: integrity, slow / feminine energy, crusade against bro marketing, growing blissfully. I tend to talk about those more on social media, however.

For Sleep Like A Boss, my main strategic pillars used to be: sleep hygiene, hormones, food sensitives and nutrition, gut health, hair mineral analysis.

Usually, you should have 3-5 strategic pillars for your business. You can even give them a name! That's your method name. For me, that's my **Impact With Integrity** method. You can also call it a blueprint or a system or a strategy.

Your pillars are also amazing for SEO (*see Chapter 3.1*). Turn them into hashtags to use on your socials!

Establishing those pillars (Five main ones and for each four sub pillars) gives you enough topics for a whole year!

Ask your audience what questions they have and use those for content ideas.

Resources to get organized and distribute:

- notion.so
- Fiverr
- Anchor.fm
- Storyblocks
- Medium (awesome to repurpose your blog)
- Canva Pro (for graphics)
- Otter.ai (transcribing text)
- missinglettr

Top tip: If you want to look more professional but are using your phone to record videos, add a little mic by Shure, pop it into your phone and the sound quality is so much better.

Repurposing your content.

Identify what your zone of genius is. Is it writing, making videos, speaking? Once you know that, you make that your first piece of content and then make mini versions (or clones) of that. So, for me, I do video only, I upload the whole thing into Dropbox and let my freelancers do the rest. But I didn't always have those (believe it or not), so here's what happens next:

Take the mp4 video file and put it on YouTube. Then, put it through anchor.fm to get the audio and you'll be on Spotify, Apple, iTunes, etc. Third, is text. I hate writing, really hate it (haha, I know I'm writing a book). So, I pay someone to take notes and deliver a condensed version. I have someone who charges $5 bucks for 15 minutes of audio.

Who to hire?

Once you've chosen your favorite medium, you can hire out the rest:

- Hire someone to take notes
- To design your graphics
- To post / schedule these on social media
- For Pinterest
- To edit videos
- Copywriter for your newsletter

Blogging: The good, the bad, the content.

From tips on quilting to financial advice you will find millions of blogs. Literally. That may sound like an exaggeration, but according to *Hosting Tribunal* over two million blogs go live every day. A record high of 77% of internet users read blogs – it's the ideal platform to convey your message!

There are many ways to monetize your blog, use it to drive traffic to your website, even turn it into a business. Sell a product or provide a service? Start a blog. Want to promote a brand you love and get paid for it? Start a blog. Have a website you want to drive traffic to? Start a blog!

Keep in mind also that you will always own the content of your blog, as it is hosted on your website, whereas your YouTube channel, social media, and podcasting could be taken away, along with all your content. Maintaining a blog and building your email list through that medium will ensure that you always have access to your audience.

Organic traffic.

Consistent blogging will help make your site searchable on Google (and Google loooves consistency) leading to organic traffic. Someone searching for information that you provide in your blog may stumble upon your blog from a Google link attracting new followers and potential customers you may never have reached otherwise – for free! From your blog you can use a call to action link offering up a freebie (*see the chapter on blogging and funnels in this section*), which leads the reader to leave their info for your email list. So the goal here is that this new person will find your blog informative and interesting enough to check out your social media (podcast and/or YouTube channel) and the rest of your website. You now have a new potential customer who is familiar with your business. Yay!

Also, check out my YouTube channel where I have more amazing free content:

https://www.youtube.com/c/ByChristineHansen/videos

Authority.

Posting long-form, high-quality, valuable blogs consistently will prove that you are THE BOMB (aka a leading authority in your field). Address common questions in your blogs, and people will begin to reference your blog intuitively. This is how blogging builds trust with your readers, so whether you are promoting a brand or selling your own product or service, your audience will be more inclined to purchase from you because you have gained their confidence.

Enhance your content strategy.

Blogging is a great way to enhance your content strategy, offering up news and promotions and information that your audience craves. Your blog will be seen as THE go-to when looking for certain solutions. When you create email funnels or post promotions and discounts, your audience and prospective customers will already have knowledge of your business making it more likely they will purchase from you. Others in your industry will look to you for current news and updated content potentially sharing and linking back to your blog. Potential business partners will see you as a leading expert in your field and be more inclined to work with you.

Shareable content.

Writing a blog will increase your chances of reaching a new audience when a reader shares your information and links back to your blog or website. You can also plug your blog in your own social media and ask others to promote it on their social media or appear as a guest on podcasts. Contributing to a guest blog and collaborating with others in your field or a field that compliments yours is also a great opportunity to share your blog website. Share articles within your blog that help promote your website or share news about products you endorse. All these plugs lead back to your ultimate goal of promoting your brand and gaining and maintaining customers.

Email list.

Having a call to action in your blog will entice readers to click and submit their information, which will grow your lead list. A call to action should promise a freebie like an eBook, whitepapers, or templates. The beauty of growing your email list this way is that it works as a sort of "set-it-and-forget-it." Readers can stumble upon past posts and by responding to your very appealing CTA, you have just secured another lead, all while doing nothing (except, of course, writing your next amazing post). Think about it: if each post you write is another way to generate leads, then all your old posts, called compounding posts, will continue doing so even while you sleep!

Supports your media pitches.

One of the goals of blogging is to reach new people to invite into your digital home so that you can connect with them. Reaching out to fellow bloggers is a great way to touch a new audience. Having a blog presence makes it easier for other bloggers to see you as a true expert and endorse you to their audience.

Repurpose blog content.

You can use your blog posts to beef up your social media presence. You can tease the blog post on social media directing visitors to your site. Give your followers a snippet of the blog content, then promise new information on a product or offer up exciting new updates if your audience visits your blog. If you have a podcast or YouTube channel, you can rewrite your blog to fit these mediums. On each platform be sure to have an alluring call to action directing them to sign up for a freebie on your blog site so that you can generate new leads.

See how all actions lead back to blogging?

So, is blogging worth it? I'd say so.

Cons of starting a blog.

- Time consuming

Blogging quality content is time consuming, especially for long-form content. Each blog needs to address common questions offering valuable solutions and information that your audience seeks. You may need to do a little research to find relevant topics and learn the needs of your audience. Your content should express fresh ideas while at the same time coming across as relatable and compelling. Blogging is an art form and takes practice.

- Long-term strategy

Publishing one blog isn't going to boost your digital presence or gain you any followers. In fact, your audience needs to encounter your brand at least seven times before they even consider taking action. This isn't to say you need to write seven blogs right away either. After you write a compelling, relevant, and relatable post, you must spend time promoting it. There are numerous ways you can promote your blog and we will delve into those a little later.

- SEO (see *more in Chapter 1 of this section*)

SEO (search engine optimization) is a major factor in creating a successful blog. If you want to rank high in Google searches you need to know how to do the SEO research or hire a professional.

162

SEO can be intimidating, but to understand the basics and how to find keywords is paramount for organic growth. SEO is certainly not the be all, end all. It is helpful but could also change on a dime. So, spend time learning about SEO, but know too, that there are other ways to gain traction.

Pro blogging tips.

- Be consistent

Consistency is two-fold. You must write consistently for your blog to gain any traction and you must remain consistent in your voice and style. Consistency in both aspects sets the tone for whether you will gain your readers' trust, and they will see you as relevant and professional. If you are not committed to banging out at least three to four blogs a month, your audience will forget about you. If you are not consistent in your voice (and this goes for all platforms), your audience will be confused and find you unrelatable. Consistency is key. Consistency will garner you more potential leads and represent your business as professional and trustworthy.

- Quality over quantity

With that being said, don't just turn out crappy content week after week just to have blog posts. Consistency applies here too

163

as your posts need to be consistently full of quality and valuable substance. Your content should answer common questions, be well written and free of grammatical errors, relevant and relatable. Your posts must stand the test of time. Afterall, years down the road a new reader could stumble across your very first post, and you want this reader to still resonate with it and become a potential lead.

- Quality images

Seems counterproductive to create an amazing blog post (that will surely be shared by every reader) just to have some random, cheesy stock photo from the internet. Choose your photos wisely. Choose photos that represent your brand and personality.

- Promote your blog

Derek Halpern from *Social Triggers* proposes the 80/20 rule: spend 20% of your time writing your blog and 80% promoting it. The ways to promote your blog seem endless, but here are some tried and true ways:

- Email- Send an email blast to your list promoting your new blog post.
- Social media – this is a no brainer. Make a post about your new blog post. Announce it on your podcast or YouTube channel. Ask fellow blogger friends to make a shoutout.

- Network: Find networking sites to connect with other bloggers in your field. Follow and comment on their blog posts. Build a relationship with them and they will return the favor. Their followers will start to notice you and visit your site.

- Consider using ads. Promote important blog posts through Facebook or Google ads.

- Long-form is better. Lengthier posts will get better results through Google searches. Consider writing most of your blogs from 1,500-3,000 words so they will get noticed on Google.

Biz Bomb

Easy Ways to Create Content Topics

1. After each client session, I take quick notes on the questions asked. Even on the really obvious ones! It's an excellent way to get ideas and see where the problems are.

2. After a year of making content, don't worry about repeating yourself – nobody's going to go back and check your old stuff. Literally, nobody. And you'll have learnt new things to add.

3. Google keyword search: see what people search for using the Google search bar and use those suggestions for your content.

4. Check out **answerthepublic.com.** Type in search terms, two sets of data: all questions.

5. Buy magazines, get inspiration.

6. Blog about your continuous education and your own aha moments.

Short-term Content: Social Media

Creating a Social Media Ecosystem for Rapid Content Creation with Jamie Palmer

In this section I'm going to talk about something really cool that I got to know through the awesome Jamie Palmer on building your own social media empire. Okay, not quite: your social media ecosystem. But listen, it's pure gold.

Jamie defines a social media ecosystem as diversifying, by using different types of social media. Follow her four top tips to build an amazing ecosystem.

1. Be really specific about your audience – who are they?

2. Ask yourself how you can make their life better?

3. Stop selling. Provide value. Show up.

4. Find groups where your ideal client hangs out.

Ideal client content.

- Jamie's top tip for that first call with a potential client: Make post-it cards with the questions they ask and create content out of that for them.
- Don't reinvent the wheel – use one content creation (i.e., video) and make it into a blog post, an email, an Insta post.
- If you run out of topics to post about, ask people (i.e., in your FB group) what they want to know.

Insider tip: Start with two social media platforms (email should always be included) and work your way up from there.

> *'Structure will set you free.'*
> **Alex Sharpens**

Use one Facebook Live to create lots of content within an hour. *(See the next section for more on Facebook Live.)*

When I used Jamie's strategy, I saw a 600 % increase in traffic to my website. Is that a result, or what!

Here is an example of her framework:

- Do a Facebook Live.
- Upload to YouTube.

- Embed in your website
- Transcribe audio from video, go through (or have an assistant go through) to check for mistakes. That's a blog post and newsletter.
- Use a scheduling software to generate snippets that you can schedule in newsletters throughout the year.
- Make a graphic for Pinterest.
- Use Wavve to make sound cards for Insta.

Facebook Live Strategies to Grow Your Business

Facebook Live is streaming live video onto your Facebook page. You really should have a business page on Facebook as a business owner. Here's mine: *https://www.facebook.com/ christinemeansbusiness* That way, you can educate and deliver value via live video.

Yep, it's scary. It's not going to be comfortable in the beginning. **You. Will. Look. Awkward.** You just need to dive in and do it.

Facebook wants to be known for live video and will push it. They push it over pre-recorded video. It's just worth it.

Video is amazing to build relationships and trust. You can be yourself, visually connect with others, they literally are looking into your eyes.

Everybody loves video.

Too scared for video? Here are my tips.

- It doesn't need to be complicated. Use your iPhone; it doesn't have to be perfect.

- BUT consider who your audience is. If you want to sell high end (like me), your video does kind of need to reflect that. I invested in a cheap kit from Amazon, lighting, etc., and it makes all the difference

- Don't look at how many people are watching. Don't look at the comments. See someone drop off? You don't know why people stop watching. And you know what? It doesn't matter! It matters what happens afterwards. People will see the video in their feed later.

- Get a teleprompter app. Start with a script.

- Practice. Record yourself. Take the recording, put it into Google and use Google voice to do a transcript (or use software like rev.com, temi.com or otter.ai). And then you can put it into your teleprompter app and just read it! Read it naturally, of course.

- You don't have to go pro from the get-go.

- Set up a fake page to practice.

- If you don't want to schedule a live video every week – if that thought makes you feel nervous – just take one day and shoot all your videos at once. Use different outfits and locations to give the appearance of different videos.

It doesn't need to be fancy. It's about the content. It's about value.

Insider tip: The videos that convert the best on Facebook are vertical, not horizontal.

Which topics to cover.

- Hold a weekly Q & A on your Facebook page and then answer those questions in your live video! If you don't have a big enough following and don't get enough questions, just listen to what your clients are saying. Hear the questions they ask and use them for topics.
- Check what's on the news. What's trending. Pick up on what people are saying about your topic.
- Sign up for Google Scholar alerts, and you get the newest articles in your topic in your inbox.
- Don't be afraid to use the same topic twice! People have to hear things multiple times for it to sink in. Plus, not the same people are going to be watching all your videos!
- Don't hold back. Say everything you can to educate.
- Every other video, do a clear call to action: ask your audience to check out your blog, website, or sign up to email for a freebie.

The foremost idea is to give.

How to position your product in the video.

You don't want to be an old-fashioned advert, right? There is a way to kindly preset your product (course, service, etc.). Start with valuable content. Present your topic. Help them understand this is a problem or that they have that issue. And then you want to deliver great content. Weave in a story of yourself or a client who had that issue. And then show how you or your client was able to overcome that problem. People will see: *OMG, maybe you can help me!* Lead into the pitch: *Now you know, you have this problem, you might be wondering how to fix it. I actually have this course or this series that can help you.* Make it easy for people to sign up, have a link, use a chat bot (see below).

Using chat bots. *(Find out all about chat bots at the end of this section.)*

You can add a chat bot to your Facebook live. People can comment with a certain word you give them and then the chat bot sends them a freebie (that particular function may not be available globally anymore due to marketing regulations). It's a powerful tool. Facebook messenger is on people's phone. They don't have to go to email. They get a notification. Messenger bots have a higher open rate (80 %) versus email (20%).

It is, however, more invasive. You do need to ask permission.

Equipment.

- Get a good webcam. (I have Logitech.) You want to look good, right?
- Get a tripod.
- Get a good mic. (I have a Blue Yeti.)
- Get good light.
- Use a filter that smooths you out.

Extra tip: Want to invite someone onto your video from your phone? Go live and tap "view" and you can add someone to the video.

Be professional but also be yourself.

TOOLBOX

Ecamm software. Use for solo videos.

Zoom. Use for Interviews.

BeLive.

Streamyard.

Succeed on LinkedIn & Create Human Connection

Believe it or not, people are actually friendly on LinkedIn! If you're going to be on a business platform, look for the business mirror image of yourself. LinkedIn is all about that human connection. One aspect of life and business you can't automate, it's the human connection.

Network, trust, connection.

3 things that every single businessperson needs to look at:

1. The demographics depending on your business (where are your people hanging out).
2. The network you can grow.
3. The money mindset of the people hanging on that platform (although that is quite assumptive, so let's be careful with that).

Demographics of LinkedIn in contrast to Facebook and Instagram:

Average age Facebook + Insta is 18-29. LinkedIn: 30-55 years old. Insta has the highest rate of fake accounts to reals accounts across social media. LinkedIn allows 30,000 organic, free connections. Average income of Facebook and Insta users: $30,000 a year. Average income on LinkedIn: $100,000 dollars a year. LinkedIn is the only platform where you can search for your ideal client in specific city, country, province.

Content:

LinkedIn Live: 10-minute video. The idea with LinkedIn is to create one piece of content a day. That content comes in 3 forms: post, video, article. What people look for: how-to, tips, motivation, inspiration. No selling, offering, product pictures.

Sell less, connect more.

The magic formula for good content: 4-6 lines of your own content that relates to what you're speaking on. Use hashtags: you're notified if you have a trending hashtag. People can find you more easily. Call To Action: ask the audience to engage. *What are your thoughts on...?*

4 key aspects to LinkedIn:

1. **Profile**. The more filled out you can make your profile the more visible you are. People use the search function on LinkedIn like they would Google. So, if you're a business coach, you need to have the term "business coach" in your profile.

2. **Searching and connecting for your avatar**. What industry are they part of, job title, etc.?

3. **Messaging.** When you start out, you'll get really bad messages.

A 3 key formula to a very good message: Authenticity. State the person's name. In the body of the message, state why you're connecting with them without asking for anything or selling. Finish with a call to action: Ask how you can support each other on LinkedIn.

4. **Network.** When you curate the right network, and post on a consistent basis, you'll be speaking directly to that network. Everything needs to be directed to the mind of the end user. Not what you want to post, but what will speak to them.

Top tip: Don't underestimate the workload. People are super helpful, but you can easily get lost. Because you have to show you're engaged. It's a bit like high school: where you have a couple of big guns and everybody wants to be their friend.

Engage with content if you like it, if you don't, don't.

Treat LinkedIn like a 401K retirement fund. Where people get lost is treating LinkedIn like a lottery ticket. LinkedIn is compounded interest over time. You have to make daily deposits to create the compounded interest of income that eventually will create your wealth. Doing things without getting anything in return.

Biz Bomb

Top Tips for Your Instagram

Disclaimer: Instagram is changing all-the-freakin'-time! Here are some tips that should be evergreen though. (Fingers crossed!)

Optimizing your Instagram bio for your ideal client.

1. Your name: it's searchable. It's a searchable term. When you're new it doesn't make too much sense to put your name there. Put your first name and then something people might be searching for. *Christine – business coach.*

2. Description: many people are not clear enough. Don't list hobbies. Make it solution-based and action-based. What is the problem you can help people with, what is the solution to their problems? Be very specific so you grab your ideal client's attention.

3. Make sure you have a strong call to action. E.g., tell them: DM "start" to learn more. Tell people EXACTLY what to do. In your bio have a specific link, not just your website, but your page with your freebie, or link to your newest YouTube video, or a link to a linktree i.e. a page with a menu (I use something called Tap bio).

TOOLBOX

Upgrade Your Instagram with Tap Bio

On Instagram (as I'm sure you know) you can only
have one clickable link in your bio. That link is prime
real estate. You can use Linktree or have a link to a
page on your website where you make sure to have
different links. OR you use Tap Bio for which you can
get different cards (much like with Insta stories). A
card is like a story page which you can build. You can
have one for your bio (picture, bio, social icons). You
can have one like a mini landing page with email sign
up form. You can have a page with one call to action
button. You can also integrate YouTube as well. There
are also cards to add posts from your Insta feed and
one to collect images to sell courses or products.

Create Great Content & Market Yourself on Instagram

If all else fails, refer back to your methodology and your pillars
that allow for variety and expertise. You can come up with
content categories. Other fillers could be categories such as: how-

to, unboxing, behind the scenes, interviews, testimonials. Come up with content types: still imagery, video, carousels. Graphics, animations, gifs. Use colours.

People connect with humanity. They want to see you.

You need to draw people in. Use photos of yourself. People trust friends, people they know. So let them get to know you. People don't trust businesses.

Top tip: Go back to your values: figure out what your pillars are. Write them on post-its and put them up around your desk.

Focus on content you can do well.

If you don't want to do video, don't. You can also do video without showing your face, where people just hear your voice.

The difference between video on Insta story and IGTV and Insta live? IGTV is Insta/Facebook's answer to YouTube/YouTube Live. IGTV lets you go longer and deeper than stories.

Insta insider tips.

- You don't want others to know whether you watched their story? *(Hello, ex-partner stalking session.)* If you go on Insta stories you can see who has seen your story. To avoid that click on the story circle after the one you want to see, swipe back a little bit and you can see the previous one without them getting notification that you've seen it.

- Mute stories without unfollowing someone: go onto their circle and hold and select mute.
- Use Insta stories for promotional push or for fun. Use the ability to see who watches your stories to customize and optimise your content.

My Insta feed is my digital business card.

Think about reaching your audiences like this: Instead of spraying the whole field with water, drip water your apple trees right at the roots. Only worry about reaching those people who will care.

Tailor and target.

TOOLBOX

How to Decide What Social Media Content to Create

Principle for social: if your editorial content is boring you, it's boring your audience. Heavily branded content is not working = when you're creating a social post and you've got too much branding vs a small icon at the bottom. If it's heavily branded it doesn't hit that human connection point. Be attune to your audience and remember it can shift. The world is constantly shifting.

Use your own triggers and interests, don't guess what your client wants.

Journaling prompt: jot down anything that is triggering you, behaviours, comments, situations, aha moments, new things you've learned.

Insider tip: Sign up for Google Scholar alerts to get the newest articles on your topic. Use a trending topic to create content.

Don't worry about repeating yourself.

Tips and Tricks

7 Ways to Gain Customers - at any stage in your Business

Let's get real, the first 2 years are hard when setting up your own business. For me, I had an advantage because I started with YouTube immediately, that came naturally. (Check me out: https://www.youtube.com/c/ByChristineHansen/videos) With my academic background, I was used to doing research with Google, and I have just also always loved marketing. But here are some things I've learned and want to share.

Don't hire someone to do everything right from the start, even if you have the funds. Because if someone you rely on quits, you would not be able to run your business. If you want to be your own boss in the online world, there's just no way around learning the ropes (and then outsourcing them).

You have to find a way to like the business side. Once you learn the tech basics you can figure out any platform.

But most importantly, don't neglect client acquisition in the beginning.

Something that's often neglected in the beginning is client acquisition. You're so busy with admin and filing, etc… but that doesn't get you clients.

Consistency in your content.

Consistency is key in content. Your online presence needs to be consistent otherwise you lose trust. Cultivate a healthy mix between eternal, long term content and short term, social media content.

1. **Forever content or evergreen content**. Refer to earlier chapters in this section to see how I use both. This is the content that has staying power. A blog post on your website, for example. It doesn't have to be a text, it can be a video, notes, etc. Aim to publish a minimum of once a month. Ideally, once a week. It doesn't have to be made specifically for the blog. You can transfer content from one place to another – e.g., upload your YouTube video onto your blog. If you don't have a website, you should post content onto evergreen platforms, such as YouTube or Pinterest.

2. **Social media**. Be strategic. TikTok, Instagram, Facebook. Personally, I mainly use Insta. Keep a healthy balance between helpful content and letting people know about

your offers, and how you work with people one-on-one. You need to guide them towards working with you. Have one in three or four posts in which you let people know how to work with you or where they can get a freebie or tiny offer. Posts are almost never just a promotion; they should still provide valuable content. If you only do promotional content, the algorithms are going to know, and you will not reach a lot of people.

3. Structure your post by teaching something first and then have your offer at the end. Or, wrap a promotion into a story. Say: *when I work with my clients, I see xyz all of the time, x being this, y being this, z being this. I created my offer that helps with exactly these 3 points.*

People who follow you should know what you do and how to get it.

4. **Podcasts**. Podcasts are super helpful in getting the word out. Being a guest on other people's podcasts is gold. Be helpful and use other people's audiences. Pitch to podcasts at least once a month. Start with small podcasts. When you pitch don't just talk about yourself. Think about how it will benefit the show and their audience.

5. **Facebook groups**. Engage in Facebook groups, not only your own. Obviously, DO NOT try to poach

other people's clients. Do not promote unless you get permission. But you can go into a group and give advice. Be authentic. Answer questions. People will go and check out your profile. Make sure your profile says what you do and who you are.

6. **Guest blog posts**. Could be for personal blogs or online magazines. Great for Google. Pitch posts once a month. Also great for building relationships with people who have a related niche but are not your competition. Consider collaborating on projects, training, video series, etc. (See point 7.)

7. **Collaboration**. Summits, interviews, blog posts, Facebook groups, expert rounds, Insta live. Do it if possible once a month. Your outreach will not always be successful but that ask should be done once a month.

8. **Newsletter / email list**. It doesn't matter how many people are on your list. Don't forget about it. Your newsletter can be a short version of other content or you can create fresh content (and even repurpose that for social media). It can be really short. The point is to keep people reminded of your presence. And, from time to time, you can offer them something. The people who are on your newsletter are ready or at least aware to buy.

9. **Workshops**. In person if possible. Reach out to companies, associations that you can give a free 45-minute talk to.

They can also be done online. You can also do workshops just for your email list. The goal is to teach people who you are and how they can work with you.

Building your business.

It's not possible to build a business in 90 days. It just isn't. Ignore anyone who says they can teach you how. **Implementation takes time**. That's all there is to it. It takes time to try things, tweak them, make them better, to achieve consistency. It takes time to get enough content online so people find you everywhere.

Your business is a living, breathing thing.

It'll take a year to really see the traction and results of your work. In the beginning, you will feel like no one hears you. That's why it's so hard. **You. Have. To. Keep. Going.**

You're paving the road for when people find you.

Top tip: Hiring a coach is a great way to speed up your results.

Journal for ideas.

I personally would not tell anyone to have a content schedule. I think you should communicate when you have something to say, when you truly want to serve your people. It's not just about you

– it's about when what you are thinking and learnt can benefit them. A great way to never run out of ideas is to write down when something triggers you or upsets you or excites you. Make a list of these moments and use them for your posts. They are always genuine. Something will happen every day that will make you ponder.

TOOLBOX

Listennotes.com

A podcast search engine. I love being on podcasts or having PR do the heavy lifting for you, to get new clients. It's a great way to get your name out there. If you simply go to iTunes or wherever and search for podcasts and then pitch to those, Apple will show you the ones that are already popular which means you will be handling a lot of competition when you pitch. On Listennotes you can find tons of different podcasts with just one keyword. I would look for podcasts that are still on the air, obviously, but I would look for smaller podcasts first that are quite new or have not received so many reviews yet. Start there to practise and build yourself up, and then you can go to the bigger shows with the smaller ones as credentials. You can even use snippets of previous interviews.

Biz Bomb

Podcasts

Podcasts are super popular and with over two million podcasts to listen to, there are 16 million avid listeners per month, according to Nielsen, and that's accounting just for the US.

One of the major benefits of podcasting is that your audience can listen anytime, anywhere. They can listen in their car, on the bus, cleaning their house, or working out. Podcasts and listening to your voice also feel personal to listeners. When a listener downloads your episode each week, they begin to connect with you, build trust and continue coming back for more information.

Podcasting can also be inexpensive. You don't need much or the most expensive equipment right away. If you have a good story to tell and stay consistent, you can easily create a successful podcast. However, since podcasts are audible, it's not as easy to make it searchable on Google. So actively promoting your podcast helps if you already have a social media presence or an established following.

However, you need to be absolutely clear on the fact that podcasting is a long-term marketing strategy. People want to come back each week and will devote hours listening, so you must be ready with plenty of quality content that usually takes days to record and edit. There is also the risk that your audience will get easily distracted and tune out, especially if your story doesn't keep their attention. So be mindful of that.

Biz Bomb

What You Need to Create Amazing Video Content

The truth? Not much. You can just use your smartphone. It doesn't need to be perfect. In fact, the less perfect, the better. People want to see the real you.

Zoom is a great way to record videos. You can get a decent camera, but a smartphone is usually good enough. However, if you want to run the video through your desktop (it's much easier to engage with comments that way), you do need a good camera.

Tech tip: Camera: Logitech G PRO X. Mic: blue Yeti Nano.

TOOLBOX

InShot App

When I make a regular video with my camera that is horizontal it's not that great for Insta stories. But what I can do is use the InShot app to change the canvas to iPhone screen style and you can change the background. It'll look professional.

Best bit? The app is free.

Top tip: If it wants to add the logo, click on it, it'll ask you to remove and you just do that every time!

Biz Bomb

YouTube

The first YouTube clip was made in 2005, and by 2006 the platform was serving upwards of 100 million videos a day, and it hasn't slowed down since. Today there are 37 million YouTube channels, and it is the second most popular social media platform with over two million users. Here is mine: youtube.com/bychristinehansen

The great thing about YouTube is that you can use its algorithms to make your website more searchable on Google. YouTube marketing boosts Google searches which will inevitably send more traffic to your site. Another positive of YouTube is that you can convey your message in a quick clip which serves well for fast-paced, content hungry people with little time or attention span.

YouTube also makes it easier for the viewer to click to your website. As they have to watch your video via phone or computer, they will have access to clicking a call to action button or navigating directly to your website. But on the flipside, viewers must have the availability to sit and watch a video and your message must be quick and to the point to consider the busy lives of your audience.

Another downside to YouTube can be the production process if you want it to look and feel professional.

Biz Bomb

How to smash your reach on Facebook

Before you post, use a point scheme to engage with others: like=1; reaction=3; heart=5; comment=3; thoughtful comment=5. People see more of your stuff when they reply to your comments on your post. Genuine interest makes people reciprocate. Only engage with posts you like (don't do this for clickbait.) Try to reach say 50 points before you post on your own page. Do something similar on Instagram: engage with 7-10 photos before writing your own post. Choose your target market time (when are your clients most likely to be online?) Then go online with an hour (or so) to spare to engage with others (ask questions etc.), and then post yourself.

Chatbot Checklist

What is a chatbot? It's an autoresponder: the user gets an automatic response on your website or page.

- Chatbot open rates: 90% (email: 20/30%)
- Rules/best practice: don't message more than every 2 weeks max.
- Give your chatbot a personality so people realise it's not you they're talking to.

You need disclaimer messages for your bot.

1. Welcome
2. Would you like to sign up for messages.
3. I'm not a doctor disclaimer (if you're a health coach). If clients don't acknowledge they can't go further.

You can deliver a whole programme through a bot. You can give them access to a library of videos through the chatbot. Only the people who've signed up to a programme can access videos as part of that programme through the chatbot.

Use the bot as the good conscience of your client: Send them a daily message asking how did you do with your sleep hygiene last night?

How do people get out of the chatbot? Hamburger menu: option to unsubscribe or add keywords to unsubscribe.

Top tip: Instead of having a link in your profile to your website, take them into your bot.

Build your network.
You are your business.

4. Planning

Section 9

PLANNING

At the end of 2019, I had this great workshop where we were planning all of 2020. It's great to have a plan and a calendar where your whole year is set down. (I run that workshop every year in December. Stalk me for more info!) The first thing I tell people is to put down their holidays! Family holidays, school holidays... My rule of thumb is that every six weeks I need to take at least one week if not two to three weeks off. I'm super religious about that.

The second thing I do is add all the private events, etc. that I have going on.

Then, I look at the projects I have for the coming year and make sure they're not scheduled too close to each other.

But in 2020, everything was turned upside down *(hello, global pandemic)*. I had planned my travel retreats and everything was booked: the villas, the excursions, spa treatments… and then the pandemic hit. And two main streams of income of around $50K were just… gone. In these kinds of situations, you need to be able to pivot and change direction and not dwell on it too much. Read on to find strategies and practises to help you plan your business.

Your Strategy

7 Steps to Creating a Content Plan

Before we get started on the 7 steps, remember: You should always communicate what you're **passionate** about, not what you think your clients want. Believe me, it'll make everything so much easier.

> *You want your business to be a content (CONtent and conTENT) empire.*

You're probably already creating content without knowing it – through Insta, Facebook Live, and so forth. Having a strategy angle to your posts is the differentiator between a strategic content strategy and one that's more willy nilly. I'll show you what's what in this chapter. Either way, if you're in business you're very likely already creating stuff.

Remember: Content is how Google will find you and send you clients for free!

How to leverage content to make money and attract clients.

One of reasons why you might be resisting doing a formal blog post or video is because you might be trying to write about the wrong thing. Or, of course, you're being lazy and then you just need to hire someone, duh, and welcome to my world (*go to Chapter 2.4 on hiring*).

But seriously, content is the way to clients, so why wouldn't you want to do it?

Consider your social media content; that's where you'll find hints and clues as to what you might want to write about and should be writing about. It all comes down to the right topic. **Find that juicy intersection between what your clients are interested in and, most importantly, what you want to write about.** Create a business that's aligned from that point and you're never going to be stuck for content. And you know what? It's much more fun to write about stuff you care about.

1. **How to strategize?** Ask yourself what was easy last month and take that data and use it to strategize the next month. Celebrate your goals and wins, take a moment to honour them and give them space.

2. **Choose a promo focus for the month**. A group coaching programme? One-on-one? Make an intentional decision of what you're going to sell. If you want to sell everything, you're shooting yourself in the foot. Or if you don't want to sell at all, well, you might want to reconsider being in business!

   You can easily prepare for creating fresh content every month. As you reflect on last month, you can make changes to what didn't work so well. You will see that some products will perform better than others and then you can scrap what isn't working. Focus on selling one thing a month.

3. **Look at your calendar,** look at the coming month, add in your business and personal activities. These are things to always consider because you don't want to be planning a launch when you're on holiday!

   Consider how long it took you to create that blog post / video and dedicate at least the same amount of time to promoting it.

   I do bi-weekly posts for my two companies. That's around 8 pieces of content a month. I batch my content, so I take a day to do it. (Yes, I'm even wearing the same outfit in my blog videos over months. Oops. Don't believe me? @bychristine_hansen.)

I'm someone who creates the whole thing in a week and then wants to tell the whole world. I get a flash of creativity paired with momentum of energy – I'm a generator – and I just go and produce.

You want to show up consistently. Also, when planning a launch don't go straight into it, do a pre-launch. Prime people for the offer. People need to anticipate. People need to be nurtured.

4. **Topic brainstorm.** All content needs to relate to the thing we're selling that month. Make a mind map with the promo in the centre and then think what themes, questions, topics does this cover? Then come up with specific questions you can base content around. You can also ALWAYS repurpose old material. For Sleep Like a Boss, I use material from 2 years ago, the same questions come up again and again. I polish them up and post.

   Top tip: You can also use articles from other publications as springboards for your content.

5. **Monthly overview.** For each week, I ask the following questions:

a. What is the blog post, the topic?

b. What is the call to action for that? Freebie?

c. The last week of the month is a great time to send out invitations for your offer.

d. How am I selling this week? What are the emails, personal outreach, targeted ads?

e. How am I attracting and getting content in front of a new audience?

f. How am I getting it in front of existing audience?

It's a nurture and engage infinity loop.

It's all about that mindset shift: if you're thinking about a month ahead, you're expecting that people will and are following you. It's much healthier for your stress levels to assume that you have a loving and interested audience. You also have to take responsibility for the people who are willing to give you their email to provide them with content. Don't be disrespectful.

Don't let yourself be fooled by a number (i.e., that of your mailing list). I had very small list for Sleep Like a Boss because people just went straight to my website to book a call and didn't make it any further on my website.

If you show up like you already have the number you want, you will work towards that number.

6. **Planning.** It's time to put pen to paper, draft notes, outline content.

1. Draft a plan: Write your topic at the top. Choose a working title. Write down answers to two sets of questions:
2. What is the purpose for my reader? What are they going to learn? Why do they care?
3. What is my purpose for this piece? What is its call to action?

Then consider what the questions are for this post and remember that they have to serve the two purposes above. Focus on answering those questions.

Top tip: If you don't like writing (like me), you can speak your text. I use otter.ai or rev.com to generate a transcript that I can clean up or get an editor to do that.

Interview yourself. Treat it like a podcast interview. You're a star!

7. **Publish!** Pull the trigger.

   Nothing converted like the moment when I started to implement content regularly. No course, training, etc. works like content creation. You do have to be patient; it can take 3-6 months to get the process moving. And then it's there for eternity. A never-ending, grateful thing.

Christine's Words of Wisdom

When you plan for something it's not just about seeing it in the future but also about visualizing the success it can be. When I first heard about the Law of Abundance (see Chapter 5.2 How Abundance Mindset Can Save Your Business), I realized it's all about seeing and feeling your future success and manifest it into being that way. I have actually been doing that since I was little without really realizing it. I've always imagined myself talking to others. When I became an entrepreneur, I started to imagine myself giving interviews on Oprah. So, since the very beginning, I would talk to myself and Oprah while walking my dog. Oprah would ask me questions, like: "So, Christine, you're a really successful female entrepreneur from Luxembourg, and you've had this amazing experience and now you're this philanthropist and are helping the dolphins in the Faroe Islands. You've been able to make a huge difference to these animals. How did you make all of that happen?" I would answer and have a talk with Oprah. It wasn't until I talked to my coach, and she said you're actually visualizing what your success will be like, that I realized what I was doing. What can I say, I'm pretty awesome even when I'm not trying.

I encourage everyone to do this whether it's on Oprah, Ellen, or an interview for Entrepreneur. That is how you can visualize and manifest your future and MAKE IT HAPPEN.

Biz Bomb

Easily Create Long-term Content for a Year with these Scheduling Tips

This is where you get super organized. Schedule a whole year for your blog posts. Trust me, it'll be a gamechanger! Blogging is so important for your business (*all about blogging in Chapter 3.3*). It gets you tracked by Google. That's all we want, right?

Remember, your website is educational, your social media is flirting.

Step 1: Count the weeks you need in a year. (I'll come back to this in a bit.)

Step 2: You need to get yourself 3 categories. 3 main bucket tags that define your business.

Now, I have two blogs for my 2 businesses: Sleep Like a Boss and Christine Means Business. Let's look at Sleep Like a Boss first. I went to a spa (best place to think) and came up with my three categories: **psychology, physiology, generic.**

Step 3: Get yourself 8 subcategories. For example, for Sleep Like a Boss mine are:

- Psychological: sleep anxiety, focused depression, resilience, creativity, dreams, feeling of falling, sleep paralysis.
- Physiological: parasites, thyroid, food sensitivity, minerals, metals, neurology, pineal glands, hormones.
- Generic: jet lag, sleep death, bedroom environment, natural remedies, supplements, naps.

I use these for my weekly blogs. I alternate sleep and business topics every other week.

For my other business, Christine Means Business, my main categories are: **mindset, marketing, branding, and copy.**

Hopefully, it should be easy to come up with topics like that for your business. Then, when you've got them down, you batch. Go back to the number of weeks you need for a year. Take one day and doll yourself up, have a shower, put on makeup, and then shoot 4 videos. That's one month of content. Or do 8 videos for 2 months. Whatever works for you.

How Planning Can Grow Your Biz by 60% with Amber McCue

When you put a plan in place for your business, you will grow 60% more than without one (research from Global State of Small Businesses Report). Listen to Amber, she knows her stuff!

Slow down to speed up.

Be intentional. Amber says, "When planning something you go into a different space with your brain, you go into that CEO mindset. Feel for growth. That CEO mindset is gold. That's where you want to be. Look at your individual months and put down your rocks, i.e., big events, trips, etc. It's not important or necessary to go into minute detail. **Get the big picture.**"

For me, it's also really important to leave some breathing space. And it's okay if some seasons are more intense for you than others, as long as you have some quiet time in between.

Be mindful. When we're intentional and mindful, it's okay to be realistic and not to have big goals all the time. Near-term goals build momentum; they're achievable. Build step upon step until we can get to the big goal. If you try to go super big from the get-go, it becomes overwhelming.

Ask yourself what's the one thing you want to get to right now –
and know more will follow.

Personally, I'm a very organic person. I'm not linear at all, which means I always have 2-3 projects going at any time. For a long time, I thought that wasn't legit because we're always taught the linear way. But I've realized it's just not the right way for me. For me, the risk is to get sidetracked. So, I allow myself to not have a linear structure, instead I bounce between projects where I have most motivation. However, I do need some kind of structure to pull me back in, otherwise everything is just all over the place!

Questions to ask yourself.

- What can you be planning for? (Events, launch, offer, list growth…)
- How do you want to live your life? (Take a break whenever you want to, according to school holidays…)
- How are you operating in alignment with the goals you have? Lot of people when they set up their own business are looking for freedom.
- How do you spend your day? Are you working at optimal times? How does your day flow?

Marketing efforts.

Amber advocates for a constant system. Ask yourself: Is your marketing working the way you want it to? If you're not getting referrals anymore, maybe it's time to rethink your marketing channels. BUT don't rely on referrals too much; it's not reliable. It's out of your control.

I find referrals so rigid; each client has their own experience of working with you. Also, you evolve. I still get referrals from the baby sleep business I had 5 years ago! People don't always catch on that you've changed. So, it can be quite disappointing. Maybe you don't offer a certain service anymore or your price has changed.

Make a revenue plan. Get intentional about where you want your revenue to come from and how to serve your clients.

Spend 2 days a week on marketing on average (not in busy seasons). Engage consistently. Be super intentional what you want to communicate.

When should you start planning?

Now, basically.

As creatives, we don't run linear businesses, but it can be really helpful to infuse some linear descriptions into our business. The sooner you plan the sooner it's going to help you to ensure results. The important thing is to give yourself permission to shift if you need to.

- Make detailed quarterly plans or even weekly plans if you can.
- Keep track of micro adjustments. Take stock constantly.
- Check in with what you want and see what you're ready for.

Christine's high road.

I am big believer in high end. But you need to be confident in what you do. Go against your gut feeling that you're not ready yet! It's okay to not be ready yet. Slow down purposefully.

Journaling prompt: write down your not-ready, half-baked thoughts and investigate the validity of those thoughts.

Actionable steps.

If you have no plan, think about your vision (even if it's not fully developed yet). Enjoy every step of the way. We might not quite know where we're going, but it'll get clearer and clearer the closer we get to it. Creating that vision – even if it's foggy – is so important.

Create your vision.

Break down your plan to 30, 60, 90 days. Sometimes even a 90-day plan is too much, especially when you're starting out. In the beginning, you have to simply try it out. Then, come back to your plan and make adjustments. Build the plan and take action.

Put those rocks (i.e., those big events) into your plan, then plan your 90 days, or even just 30. Then, work it. Every. Single. Week. Take 15 minutes every Monday or Sunday and break down your plan: These are the 3/5 things you need to accomplish this week to move closer towards your goal.

Know the feeling of your goal – that's enough.

One-Day In-Person Workshop or 4-Day Retreats: When to Hire A Planner with Jillian Smith

In this section we'll talk about how to take your workshops further.

The first step is to understand your audience. You need to know who is going to be in the room so that you can tailor the experience. You want to make your audience comfortable. Give them the sense that they're here to learn and grow.

Check out Jillian's awesome tips to make your event memorable.

The one-day workshop.

Want to plan a full-day, 8-hour workshop? Ask yourself whether it is a strictly educational workshop or whether there will be an on-site sales component. A different configuration of the room might be needed for each scenario. Will there be food or drink? There's actually science behind when to feed people and when not! Google it.

I would suggest that even if you have a one-hour workshop, you should sell something. Even if it's something for free.

Tips to take a meh workshop to an exquisite event.

Printing materials can go a long way to make an event feel personalized. Spell people's names correctly. It's all in the small touches. Greet everyone with a smile at registration. Make sure that whoever is at the registration desk has a level of emotional intelligence and training. Give your guests a warm welcome. Have special seating for VIPs. If you can provide goodies (if you're doing several events you can buy in bulk across events) that's always good. Even better, if it's shareable on social. Make your event instagrammable. Make it pretty.

Retreats.

The crème de la crème. You want the right people at your retreats who are ready to work and learn. They become your brand ambassadors because you spend so much time with them. The participants understand the investment because they get the one-on-one interaction. *I am with my coach*. Participants also lean on each other, can create human and business connections. You can also combine business and leisure to create a bi-leisure retreat. The best bit: You can still sell on a retreat: the next retreat, extensions to your current programme, the next coaching level.

You should always have the next step to sell.

Booking a location.

When choosing the venue, it's important to remember that you want to stay on site throughout. It's just so much easier to coordinate and networking also happens after hours. Those end of the day drinks? That's when the connections happen.

Contracts.

You need someone who knows contract management. Ways to negotiate room rates, etc., depending on catering and room facilities. Knowing what you can negotiate is invaluable.

How to avoid mistakes.

Not being in the loop of communications with your team is a recipe for disaster. Miscommunication or lack of communication is the quickest way to set you up for failure. Use a platform where you can all retrace your steps and communicate such as Basecamp or Asana.

Why is hiring an event planner a good idea?

As the coach you can be fully present if you have a planner. An event planner is like a support team member. It means you have peace of mind. You can just show up, be present, be great.

Finding an event planner.

You want to work with someone who works full time. Especially if you're planning a large event. You need someone who is accessible. Ask for referrals in your community. Have a conversation about what you envision and listen to what they say. They need to understand what your goals are and have your best interests in mind.

Is it worth hiring a planner for your one-day conference?
It depends. 85 % of the time it makes sense, even if it's in a

smaller venue or virtual. If you want to pitch something to your audience, your event needs to work well.

Christine's event horror story.

One day, I attended an event in London where they didn't have a planner and the room, above a pub, had not been cleaned or set up, and there was no catering. And, believe me, **if you have your clients leave with the stink of beer in their hair, you can't sell them anything.**

People invest time and money – it makes sense to treat them properly.

Top tip: A one day workshop is very powerful. Teach your method in the workshop and upsell to your one-on-one mastermind or a bespoke commitment or a retreat. It's a great piece in a funnel. Especially, if you live somewhere where people have money!

Why You Must Prioritize BEFORE You Create a Plan with Kathryn Hofer

A lot of people feel like planning is restrictive, says Kathryn. But the best part about planning is that it's flexible. Planning is freeing! Once you understand that you will see that your plan is meant to serve **you.** If we're planning properly, we're changing and adapting.

Planning gives you structure, but life rarely goes as planned!

Kathryn's 2 simple approaches to planning.

1. **The next step approach**. For those who are super creative and spontaneous, don't plan a lot. Start with the next step approach. Say you want to redo your website. What's the first step you should take? Write it down, put time in your schedule, and then do it. When you're done with that, you ask: now, what's next?

2. **The project plan**. You've got a big project (let's take the redesigning your website example again) and what you do is break it down into manageable chunks. Figure out what the end goal is and where you're headed, identify the obstacles (i.e., kids, childcare), and break down big milestones.

    *   Put together two-week sprints over a three-month period. So, the first two weeks might be doing a website audit.
    *   The next two might be mapping out the pages and their copy. (Check out the glossary for definitions.)
    *   The next two might be finding images and links etc.
    *   The last step is then to get really detailed: Within those two weeks what are all of the tasks and actions you need to do?

Ideally, you would go down to 30-minute steps. It might seem overwhelming but every time you sit down to work on your website, you just go into your calendar and tackle the next step and you know it's only a 30-minute task.

If you're overwhelmed and don't know what the steps might be, reach out to people who have done it before.

BOOK BOX

The One Thing, Gary W. Keller and Jay Papasan

They ask an amazing question: What's the one thing that will make everything easier?

Top tips.

- No time to plan? Use the 2x rule. That means if you're doing something new, always double the time you think it will take.
- If you're doing things over and over, track the time it takes you and you'll know for the next time.
- Schedule your personal stuff: holidays, things to do, etc. (See Nerd Box.)
- How to figure out boundaries? Start with less. What are the things you have to do to keep things running (also

215

called your maintenance tasks)? Start with those. Figure out how much time it takes. Kathryn suggests to take a quarter and say "no" to every opportunity. Wow. I know. It's a hard approach but it'll help you figure out your maintenance tasks. It doesn't mean no, never; it means **not now**. You can say I can't do it now, but I can do it next quarter.

- Write **experience statements**: phrases that set you up for success. Describing what you want to feel and experience in your life, rather than just a number you want to hit.

NERD BOX

Priority. The word "Priority" was singular in English language for over 500 years, not until the 1900s did it become plural. Which means that there was a shift from your priority to your priorities. But you can't really have more than one priority at any given time.

TOOLBOX

Organizing your notes with Evernote.

The Evernote app is like a shoebox, you dump everything in.

It's a shoebox you can use for receipts, invoices, etc.

The search function is phenomenal. The app looks for things related and suggests related things when you search. Did I mention colour-coding?!

It's also scannable, you can save a picture of a .doc as PDF or .jpeg.

THE golden rule: Prioritize, plan, adjust

Kathryn's life philosophy: **Progress is perfection.**

Planning for a New Year

Get the biggest calendar you can find, one where you can see the whole year, and put it on a wall in front of you. Be careful not to have too many projects. Schedule time off and mark it out! Colour-code different launches. Work in 6-week sprints.

You have to also give your email list space. Make sure you're not launching at the same time as your holiday.

Also, you can't be springing last minute things on your team! That would be super unfair. That's not good leadership.

If you're not linear (like me), just take one afternoon to get the planning done.

Some people can react really quickly and get something out that is really timely. Others (like me) need to take a bit more time and take things step by step. It's not a race. Do it in your own way.

BUT if you're the rabbit and create things really fast, be careful not to burn out. And if you're the tortoise, taking your time, make sure you don't get paralyzed.

5. Personal Development & Health

Section 5

PERSONAL HEALTH
AKA I LOVE MYSELF

I am a really spiritual person, something that took me a long time to admit to myself and this is also something I really love to see in my clients. Yes, a business has to be logical, it has to make sense, but the soul piece is really important too.

I always say that you need to connect with your soul clients – but that means you also need to figure out what your soul is all about.

Look after your soul and nurture it. If you want to show up every day for your soul clients, the first thing you have to do is look after yourself.

I love luxury, travel, and I love to connect and interact. These are the things I make time for. I plan for holidays and spending time with the people I love. And going to spas – because why wouldn't you?

We can often forget that looking after yourself is the most important first step in building a business. Everybody knows how important the premises of a shop are, right? Make sure that your lighthouse shines and sparkles. Give it a rest, a fresh coat of paint, and open the windows to new experiences once in a while.

This chapter is packed with tips and tools on how to do that.

Looking after Yourself

Maintaining Mental Health in Business (and Life)

Integrity is my essence, baby!

Integrity is a really important word for me. It really is my essence. Think back to those dreaded years of 2020 / 21. Those are a real benchmark when it comes to integrity. That time was really hard because I couldn't be integral to myself (on account of the restrictions imposed on all of us). I didn't watch any news in 2020. Nope, I literally just didn't go there. I didn't want to know numbers of cases or deaths. I didn't want to know what was going on. **This was my way of surviving.** I limited my social media, I stuck to places that are lighter (for me that means Insta instead of Facebook). I mean, looking at pretty underwear is better than comments on the next lockdown, right?

And here is what I learned from that:

Allow yourself to have a quiet moment and don't judge yourself for being lazy (although I am lazy, and I love it). In 2020, I took a lot of naps, walks, carved out space for myself, did not force myself to talk to people. It was a real test, and I actually enjoyed my lonesomeness.

If you came through 2020 kind of alright – good on you!

Here are my top tips for surviving a crisis, or even just managing day to day life. It's all in the little things!

- Find a practice that makes you feel more connected.
- It's important to have people you can talk to, the **right kind** of people.
- I love massages. Seriously. For me, that kind of thing is just as important to invest in as business classes.
- I get counseling. I have coaches. I surround myself with experts.
- Customize your feed (on socials) to what you need.

- I love myself an expensive thong. (Say what now? Yep, you read that right. It makes me feel amazing.)

Biz Bomb

Stop Waiting for Your Confidence to Show

THE mistake people make is putting off **putting yourself out there** because you're waiting for your confidence to show. But it never comes, right? You think, I still need to wait for this, I still need this, I just want to finish this.... and then I'll have confidence to go out there. Wrong! Confidence is the **last thing** to happen when it comes to learning something new. When you're brand new you're not going to have confidence. Full stop. The only way to get confidence is TO DO THE THING.

You've got to do the thing. Sorry friends, there's no magic bullet here. BUT I promise you: The more you do it, the more confident you'll feel. If you truly want to feel as confident as you can possibly be, you have to do the thing and repeat it again

and again

and again.

Having Clarity & Boundaries in Your Business-And Say No to Coffee Meetings

I mean, I love meeting friends for coffee, to have lunch, or go to a spa. But when people come at me and want to pick my brains for free, I say no. I'll tell you why you should too. But first, you need to gain clarity on what you and your business are all about. Know who you are, know your business, gain perspective. Have the right mindset before you tell people to eff off.

Top tips to keep perspective.

1. Have clarity of purpose. When you know where you're going, it's easier to pick yourself back up.
2. You need to build resilience. Negative messages build up in your brain, and it's so important to stop those when they're happening and replace them with something that's **true and honest for you.** Build up the positive side of your brain. If you can replace a negative thought with something true in the moment, then you're going to be more positive. Consider: what would your mother (or best friend or partner) think if they heard how you talk about yourself? Take yourself out of yourself and gain perspective.

> **BOOK BOX**
>
> **Katie Byron, *Loving What Is: Four Questions That Can Change Your Life***
>
> All about replacing those negative thoughts with positive ones.

I know. Your mind is not really on your trajectory when you're building a business. You're too busy running around getting all those business credentials. But believe me, that can lose you a lot of time in the long run. This step might seem weird in the beginning but it's essential. Personally, I started with oracle cards… If you're someone who is not into those things (and I wasn't in the beginning), it can feel really strange. But believe me, if you loosen up a bit about these things, you'll reap the rewards. Do whatever you need to master the mindset you need. This kind of stuff is a resilience muscle, and it does become easier. It's all about catching the negative thoughts in the moment instead of letting them fester.

If you can master the mindset work early on, you're going to go far fast.

Quick tips to mindset bliss.

- Set alarms on your phone 3 times a day and commit to 2 minutes of just mindfulness work. Taking the trash out (okay, no, that's what my man is for), deep breaths, sit with yourself. It's like going to a gym.
- Listen to those gut instincts. I.e., don't say yes to a client when it feels wrong.
- Niching works. Give your niche a shot for a year. You can't afford to go down all these rabbit holes. Have courage to stay in your line. Foster community, build a community of businesspeople / coaches / entrepreneurs / creatives and have people to refer to. It's also really confusing for you if you don't know what you're focusing on. Big plus: If you're really well-known in your space, you'll get referrals from people who don't even know you.

Imposter Syndrome.

Raise your hand and get into the arena of life every single day. Jot down opportunities you've missed throughout the week because you felt like an imposter. Catch yourself thinking this and build the muscle to notice it (like with negative thoughts). So, you might give yourself homework to speak up 3 times in a week (in meetings, for example).

You need to be your own PR person.

Nobody is going to spontaneously award your greatness. You need to tell people about it. If you want to land a certain type of client, tell everyone you know: this is the kind of client you want. The more you talk about it, the more likely it is to happen. You need to start telling people what it is you need because that's how it happens.

For me, the easiest thing to start with is giving. I invite people to my podcast, for example, and start the connection that way.

Remember: It's okay to change your mind, offering, niche, clients, etc. It's okay to change.

Setting boundaries.

When people reach out for a coffee, consider whether you really want to do that. It's a big chunk of time that you're investing if you think said people just want to pick your brains.

Similarly, when working with clients you need to be crystal clear in your contract. (This is the deal; this is when I'm available. This is when I offer additional support.) Consider adding a signoff to your email: *I'm available at this and this time / between this and this hour.*

Top tip: Write a TO DON'T list: e.g., I don't do coffee meetings.

Insider tip: The Number 1 question to write on a piece of paper and put in your pocket:

When I say yes to a thing, what am I saying no to?

Yes to a coffee meeting, is **no** to honouring people who are already paying me.

When I say **yes** to not charging enough, I'm saying **no** to my financial security.

Set boundaries from the beginning.

How to Deal with Haters & Negative Feedback

As soon as you start owning what you believe in, people start having opinions. It's just how it is. The problem is: One negative feedback can take over your world. But everyone has an opinion. So, how do you deal with it?

For me, there is no plan B. I want to keep going. When you're just starting out (because you build up your tolerance over time) one thing that can help is sharing your experience. It's difficult for people to disagree with your personal experience. You know what's working for you and why you're doing it.

Don't take stuff personally, what other people say reflects them, not you. Stuff might be happening in their life; something might have triggered them...

It takes a lot of courage to show up online and to share; the mean commenters are not doing that, they are hiding.

A while back, when I started my very first business, I was in a national newspaper in Luxembourg. It was a huge one-page spread with a huge image. There was a shitstorm when that was published. Bashing me about damaging children. I was 3 weeks into opening my business and super vulnerable. There was one person in particular who was really nasty slagging off my looks *(how mature right? *eyeroll*)*. Then, a few weeks later, I met her in person. It was so awkward; we both knew who the other was – and guess what, she pretended not to see me.

You can always choose whether to be negative or positive. So, I didn't go up to her and confront her. But: it was cathartic.

People who hurt, hurt others.

A good strategy for me is this. Negative comments go straight to the gut, right? Visualize the hook of hate people are throwing into your gut. Visualize detaching the hook and sending it to wherever you want ... a place of peace, love, God, whatever you believe in.

Talk about it to people you trust. Share it and that will make it seem less of a big deal.

Keep track of your wins. When people say nice things, take a moment to absorb it, to save it. When you get a negative comment, go back to the positives.

Let yourself feel it, and then let it go.

Choose your battles wisely.

Biz Bomb

Take a Break with the Timeout App

Need a break? Haven't left your desk in hours? Did you know you shouldn't be sitting for longer than 1 hour?

Enter the **Timeout App**: This app reminds you to take a break. And it's not just a notification, it walks across your screen, prevents you from clicking on anything for about 5 seconds. It forces you to think for a second, and that means you're more likely to take a break. You can delay the break or skip if you must. You can set up a break for 5 minutes or whatever. You can set it to once an hour or whatever you want. Try and get some movement. Lunges around the house. Get fresh air. You're going to be so much more productive, I promise.

Your Personality & Struggles are Part of Your Brand with Tracy Raftl

Don't hide your struggles. Don't worry about setbacks; they happen to everyone. Don't think because you still suffer from something means you can't talk about it or can't be an expert about it. A personal connection really helps people to relate. Let's deep dive into that vulnerability (yay) and see what can be done about it with the help of the amazing Tracy Raftl.

Honesty and being vulnerable is key.

Tracy says: *"Branding is the whole perception of what other people think of your business. Your brand should be based on your personality. But remember, it's not exactly the same thing. So, if you're lazy, maybe don't make that part of your brand in an obvious way. Except, sometimes it works (for me, for example). But not everything has to be broadcast."*

Being you makes you more attractive to your ideal client.

Tracy's top tip: Don't know how you appear to others? Work with a brand expert or ask friends and family. Ask for 5 characteristics that you feel like sums you up. Ask a few different people to get a good idea.

Your journey.

When you're new and have not shared much yet, start with sharing your personal journey. How you got here. Share it in a little more detail than you normally would. It should feel a little bit scary, a bit uncomfortable, says Tracy. **Fear is just a sensation.** If you really want to stand out, you can't give a toss about people who judge you. Once you start to put yourself out there and feel connection with people, you will start to feel the positives.

Your visual presence.

Once you know what your brand is you need to figure out how to brand. That means, what should your brand look like? What colours and fonts to use, how should your website look?

Tracy's top tips for branding:

- Imagine someone else with your brand and visualize what that brand would then look like.
- Choose colours you like but also that match your personality.
- When you're writing, think about how you would say something to a friend. Make it informal.
- What to wear (on video): you need to be comfortable. Put on make-up if you want.

- Be a nice version of you.
- Be consistent.
- Invest (or create yourself) in a brand sheet / guide. Lay out all of the colours to use, fonts, tone of voice, etc. If you have a team, it's so helpful to guide them.

Remember, branding takes time to establish.

You might want to invest in a branding specialist on a regular basis because you will change and your brand will change.

> *"Marketing is the equivalent of asking someone on a date. Branding is the reason they say yes."*
> **(Ren Jones)**

Want to hire Tracy?

Tell her I sent you and get an amazing offer!

TOOLBOX
Use This Technique to Bring Focus to Your Day

Check out Marcel Hof's 5-day Breathwork course.

Why You Need to Invest in Yourself to Grow Your Business with Kristin Hartjes

Rule number 1, says Kristin, is **understanding the value of what you have to offer**.

She has an excellent technique to overcome self-doubt and the guilt about charging money to help. *"Think about it this way. Helping people is so much more valuable than other stuff people spend money on (i.e., a TV). Right!?"*

Personally, I invested heavily in personal development. That's how I understand what my clients need. If you've never invested in yourself, you don't understand how to charge for other people to invest in you!

Now, my price point for VIPs is between $7-10K a day. Because I know what the results will be. I've done it before. I'M WORTH IT.

How do you help your clients with overwhelm?

Overwhelm happens in the brain. We can only ever do one thing at a time. Even if you're trying to multitask. Overwhelm is usually thinking what you should be doing and not focusing on the one task in front of you. Kristin advises: bring it back to simplicity. Do one thing at a time, and then move onto the next.

But this might not work for everybody. As you know by now, I'm not a linear person. So, I don't go down a to do list from beginning to end, but I do get the stuff done.

Keep it simple. Once you can breathe you can create add-ons. Start with your core project.

Self-doubt.

Self-doubt is a big issue. As Kristin points out, we think the problem is the action we're taking or that we don't have the right plan. That means you're ignoring your intuition. You have a hard time investing in yourself and getting support because you don't believe you can be successful.

Kristin points to a truth: **People say they want clients but at the same time are afraid of having clients.** It's not the action. It's the thoughts that are preventing you from being successful.

Self-doubt is a blind spot, and you don't even know you have it. That's when working with a personal development coach can make sense to recognize self-doubt and work on it.

PLUS: If you're a coach, it's really important that you've been coached yourself and have experienced that. Be on the other side so that you can see how transformational it is.

How to Overcome Imposter Syndrome with Tara Wagner

Are you struggling with who you are? Do you worry whether you're enough? Believe me, everybody (or almost everybody worth their salt) worries about these things. Let's talk about mindset with Tara – it's all in the mind, honey.

A huge portion of business success is mindset. Like, really. It's a massive part. Like 80 % mindset, 20 % strategy.

You can't build a solid business on shaky foundations.

Imposter Syndrome.

Yep, it's the dreaded Imposter Syndrome: the outward appearance of having it all together while on the inside you think you're a fraud. Example: You tell yourself; I just need one more certificate / training etc., then I'm ready to launch. Or more credits. You have a rock in your stomach, a constricted feeling in your throat / chest when thinking about putting yourself out there / going to a networking event. But on the outside, you might actually look badass. That means, you can never know who is suffering from Imposter Syndrome and that can feel isolating. That super successful business friend? She probably is.

Look, you can't be an expert without putting in the practice – it's all about trial and error. Delving into your craft.

You know what that means? Taking clients from **day one**. If we continuously think we're not there yet, it'll hold us back. If we sit in the back of the room, won't speak up, won't go after big opportunities, we can never develop our full potential. As Tara puts it: **"We end up staying small because we're playing small."**

The only way to grow is to pick up something that's too heavy.

Now, Tara has a fantastic way of looking at it: **Imposter Syndrome is an inherently selfish and self-centered experience.** Wait, what? But think about it. It is our mind saying the only thing that matters is what other people think of me.

Especially for you peeps in the health business: you're here to serve other people. It's no longer about you. You get to take yourself out of the way.

For me, Imposter Syndrome is ego. You're allowing yourself to be self-indulgent because you're taking your eyes off what really matters. Once again: You're here to serve other people.

It's a self-protection, self-preservation thing. Our ego is trying to protect us not to self-sabotage. Imposter Syndrome is the desire to be liked, to be loved. That is legitimate. Imposter Syndrome is a belief that you being liked is being threatened by showing up and not being good enough. It's a self-protection mechanism.

Tara's strategy.

Look at what your needs are. The only thing emotions are, are signals of our needs. If we're feeling anxious or afraid, it means I have a feeling that is not being met or I'm being / perceive as being threatened. If we can identify the need, the fear often goes away with it.

For most people Imposter Syndrome never goes away, but the experience changes. Imposter Syndrome is weakened, it doesn't have the same impact. It takes a lot of practice and focus. Turn the fear into excitement. Same physical reaction, same sensation. But it just means you're doing something important. The reason why Imposter Syndrome is so prevalent among entrepreneurs is because you're always pushing forward, not staying comfortable, and expanding. Things that expand you in life – marriage, parenting, owning your own business – all of those will require you to **Not. Get. Comfortable**. It's important to understand that feeling – it means you're on the right track. **Because it's the high achievers that feel it the most.**

Nothing wrong with living in the comfort zone!
But you can't do that with a business.

Tara's step-by-step strategies to beat Imposter Syndrome.

Naturally, Imposter Syndrome is unique to everyone's personality. But here are Tara's awesome steps to overcome it:

1. **Detach emotions from work**. Feelings are not facts. Observe the feelings but don't believe the feelings. Imposter Syndrome is emotional, so bringing a logical mind to the table is so important. Mentally prepare yourself. How do I deal with that? Just because you think it, doesn't mean it's true. We take in messages from when we're a child and can't distinguish between doing something bad and being bad.

2. **Digging into the experience of Imposter Syndrome itself**. Journal about it. It slows you down. Putting pen to paper gets you into the less conscious. Ask yourself: What was the situation I'm afraid of? What are the thoughts around it? How does my body feel? What are my worries, beliefs?

3. **Look at the impact Imposter Syndrome has had on you**. This is best done alone. Take time to look at where you would be in life if you didn't deal with this. It doesn't mean that it needs to be always bad. The point is to realize how much further you could be in your personal goals. Real mindset work is about doing things that don't

always feel great. Two things that motivate: pain and pleasure. Use both of them.

4. **Look at where you might be without this**. This might be too scary. That's okay. If I were to stand at bottom of a staircase and wanted to get to the top in one huge step, that would be difficult. Instead, take one step at a time. Overnight success is not real. Don't compare yourself to others who will be at a completely different stage. Learn how to compare in a healthy way. If necessary, unsubscribe from the ones you need to.

One step to do today.

Practice like crazy. Practice the mindset you want to emulate. Practicing a new habit until you develop it. If I loved and approved of myself and had no Imposter Syndrome, what would I do? How would I show up? Practice that. Mindset doesn't happen in the mind, it happens when you're hitting the pavement.

You have to make a shift when you notice things are not working anymore. If you're showing up as your best self, what would that look like? Whether it's in your pyjamas or high heels.

It's up to you what you perceive.

What you focus on is how you feel. You can create pretty much whatever personality, whatever outcome you want. It might be hard work, but it can be done.

Biz Bomb

The Secret to Pushing Through the Fear of Putting Yourself Out There

How do you overcome those cringy feelings about putting yourself out there?

Think about it this way: If you want to have impact, play bigger, help as many people as possible, you have to feel comfortable being a leader and holding space for hundreds of people. It's a responsibility that you need to take up.

If you're not doing the work, it's irresponsible to your clients. Consider what triggers you – you need to work on these things, so they don't get in the way of your work. It's not fair to your clients if you're not doing the work on yourself. Work on things you need to improve.

I'll let you into a secret: the fear does not go away!

Whenever you do something out of your comfort zone, you get the fear. Every time I do something new, I get scared, I have self-worth issues. It's an important thing to realize because what you understand is that you just have to push past it. We might not have a lot of confidence; you might not have realized you needed to put yourself out there when you started your online business. Whatever your fear is, there's no point waiting because it doesn't matter how many courses you do, etc. The. Fear. Will. Always. Be. There. The only thing to do is to push through. Don't let it hold you back.

The fear stops being an excuse for not taking action.

I acknowledge the fear when I feel it, but I don't let it hold me back. Running a business is uncomfortable. It feels weird, scary, it makes you doubt yourself. But if you don't push past the fear, you're never going to achieve the big goals that you have.

Take a moment and consider what action are you going to take this week to push past the fear? Maybe it's an email to your list, post on Insta, FB Live…

GO DO IT. At least once. When you figure out what actually works and what doesn't, only then you can remove certain marketing strategies that are not in your natural zone.

Personal Development

How Abundance Mindset Can Save Your Business

Get away from a scarcity mindset. You can have the wrong mindset because you have no money, but it can also be about how you *feel* about your money. **Self-awareness is our biggest tool.** If you feel there's an area in your life where you're struggling, that is where you need to do the work.

For example: my clients can't afford me – is this something you want to believe? If not, what would you rather believe? Focus on that. Tell yourself: I believe if they really want it, they'll make it work.

What's triggering you about it? Where are you choosing to believe that? The areas of least resistance are where we most manifest in our life / hold the most belief in.

BOOK REC

Margaret Lynch, *Tapping Into Wealth*
Joe Dispenza, *Breaking the Habit of Being Yourself*

Desire to be in that energy. The energy of someone who has the money mindset.

Money and mindset.

Shifting your relationship with money is tracking your money. Know your motives to why you buy. Usually, when you avoid facing your numbers *plus* still spend a lot at the same time it's a sign that you're trying to fill an emotional gap with buying stuff if you lose the overview of your spending.

Alternatively, when we're tracking our money we're shifting our energy around it. The more awareness we have, the more power we take back.

One of biggest problems is we're consistently tending to giving our power away: When I say "I can't afford this, people can't afford my services", what we're actually saying is there's a power outside of me greater than me. You're in a space of victimhood. Once we start observing, we're taking our power back. And at the same time, when we check our bank accounts, it can feel pretty neutral. At some point that will turn to gratitude. It's the energy shifting. What happens is how you speak.

The way you price your offer is no longer, what do I think my clients can afford, but what information do I want to offer? It changes who you attract. Confident energy attracts people who are ready to invest. You only notice 7-8 important things in a day, based on what your brain has told you is important. So, when you tell yourself something, your brain looks for proof of that so pick a few strategic affirmations to support your brain and hence your business that way.

Energy when spending money is so important. It's circulating. So be grateful when spending versus remorseful.

Do you need a coach to help you with this?

It's hard to see what's happening up close. A coach can figure out what your fake truth is. The stories you tell yourself. It can be useful to have a coach to mirror back your crap.

TOOLBOX

Struggling to Come Up with Content Ideas?
Use This Tip.
I'm not a fan of writing but talking is something I love to do. Often, I get ideas while I'm listening to music or driving my car. In that situation, what you can do is take out your phone and whip up a voice memo. When it's content batch day, just listen back to your voice memos and it will be so much easier to come up with content and inspiring captions.

Mastering Your Money Mindset

Especially at beginning of starting a business, money questions can be scary. I had a period where I simply avoided checking my bank statements at the beginning. I know, I know, don't do that.

Here's the thing: **Money is just a resource**. In the past everyone had cash, so it was easy to have an overview. There is a psychological exchange when handing over cash in exchange for something. But with a card, you're just rewarding yourself. If you feel shame about debt, remind yourself that it's normal to have debt and the industry encourages it. Change your attitude to debt: It got you your education, etc. Be grateful for what it enabled you to do.

Where to start?

- Take a step back and ask yourself why you went into business. What do I want to do with the money I'm making? You need a bigger reason why.
- Gain awareness: are you making enough money to pay the bills? Profit carries you forward. Calculate revenue according to your lifestyle. Forget generic goals. See how much you need. It's so personal. Having that number is powerful. I need to make so much a month, see how much you need to charge your clients.

- Money needs to move (like water).
- Money is neutral. Not bad not good.

BOOK BOX

- Margaret M. Lynch, *Tapping into Wealth: How Emotional Freedom Techniques (EFT) Can Help You Clear the Path to Making More Money*
- Lynne Twist, *The Soul of Money: Reclaiming the Wealth of Our Inner Resources*
- Lynne Twist, *The Soul of Money: Transforming Your Relationship with Money and Life*
- Jen Sincero, *You're a Badass at Making Money*

Check out my amazing money mindset course and bag 50% off with the coupon code "BOOK"!

https://www.christinemeansbusiness.com/mmjj

My Personal Money Block.

I was bad at math, and so I thought I was bad at money. Plus, I never had to worry about it much before in my life. I gave emotions to money. So, for example, my family's savings equalled bad money in my mind because I hadn't earned it. I had to learn that I could use it.

You can't help people if you can't pay your bills.

Actionable steps to take.

1. First step: Take a moment, close your eyes, take a deep breath, thank yourself for having these feelings and wanting to take action.

2. Next step: What does your ideal life look like? What are the feelings you want to feel in this ideal life? Images, smells. Visualise every morning what you want to achieve.

3. If you don't have an easy way for people to pay you, do that first. Second, get a way for people to book in. Make it easy for people.

4. Sit down and write down a number you want to pay yourself every month. Tally your expenses and write that down. Get a revenue calculator and put those two things in. Put them onto a post-it note everywhere around your house.

OR Go to your bank account and print off the last statement. Mark with highlighter everything you weren't using.

5. Note the difference between overconsumption and luxury. Something you buy but don't use = overconsumption. Luxury = expensive notebook I use and brings me joy.

Ask yourself before you purchase the next item. Will I enjoy it, use it, have space for it? I have spent $80 on a thong. It makes me feel amazing. I wear it to a meeting when I'm about to close a deal.

Recognize that luxuries require resources. Circle back to your goal of earning a specific number.

4 Foundations for a Successful Business with Rebecca Tracey of The Uncaged Life

It is a common mistake to invest in a logo and branding before having clear foundations. You don't have to plan and prepare 6 months behind the scenes before you launch, but you do have to start in the right place and make sure you can clearly describe what you do.

Foundation 1: Clear messaging. Why do you do what you do? What's your approach? How is this different from what other people have tried? Being clear about what makes you different is what will help you stand out.

Foundation 2: A clear niche and doing market research in that niche - stop guessing or assuming what people want, and let THEM tell YOU.

Foundation 3: Creating results-oriented packages. Don't just say: we will work together for as long as we need and on whatever issues you want.Give your message context and create packages based on the results your clients want in their lives. Clear packages help them trust that you can deliver those results.

Foundation 4: Marketing. Tell the world about what you do (with clarity). Most people go wrong and start with 4, BEFORE they are clear on how to even articulate it yet. Marketing only works once you have the first 3 foundations dialed in!

Get as clear as you can on the problem you want to solve. *(See all about niching in Chapter 1.2)* Then go and talk to as many people as you can. Take your assumptions, and find out what people are **actually struggling with.** Then, create solutions for that thing. Simple, right?

Top tip: You don't just do market research once. Do it again and again and again. You're welcome ;) Keep up to date with clients' results. Pick up on what people vent about. Pay attention to what else you see potential clients talking about and complaining about. That stuff is gold! Then you can take your market research language and copy paste onto your website - voila, amazing, compelling copy!

How to set up your offer package:

- Start by crunching numbers; figure out how much money you need a month. *(Go to Chapter 2.5 for all about pricing.)*

- Make sure your package has a start and end date. It can even be just one session, as long as you're clear what it is. **Remember—your offer should work towards a clear result.**

- Make sure to set a pricee for the whole session/the whole duration of the program (not hourly). That means you are pricing based on the value you're providing, not just the number of hours you're spending. Don't go down a rabbit hole of trying to find out what others charge. It doesn't matter as much as you think! You will find cheap people, and expensive people. Plus, you have no idea what other people's mindset about money is! Price based on what feels good to YOU, and know you can always raise your prices in the future.

- Once you have the above foundations, go and tell everyone you know about what you do! Send 30 emails to people you know letting them know specifically what you do, what problems you can help with, and how many spots you have open. Let them know you are accepting referrals if they know anyone who might be a fit! You never know who will show up in your inbox (or your bank account!) now that you have that kind of clarity.

Christine's package: I'm a big fan of tiers. I have 3 offers. I like my VIP offer (top tier) to be enough to cover all my monthly expenses. I need to make $8,000 a month and my VIP offer covers that easily. *(I talk more about pricing and packages in Chapter 2.5)*

Biz Bomb

Increase Productivity by Eliminating Reactive Tasks

Think you don't have enough time? Spend hours on all that admin?

Ever heard people say: Get rid of all your reactive tasks in the morning. Before you even have breakfast or coffee, answer your emails.

I say: Answering emails is often putting out fires. It depends on the person, but mornings are often the most productive. Consider what you might want to allocate to the morning. Maybe you want to leave emails until noon. If you get stressed by emails, don't open them until noon. Answering emails first thing puts you in a reactive state.

Knowing Your Worth, Getting Efficient & Making Money with Dr. Meghan Walker

> ### TOOLBOX
>
> Living Matrix (New York company): can have it on your site, clients can complete questionnaire. Tool to see where their body is stressed, etc.
> Livingmatrix.com

Decide on your business model.

For me, I will only ever have a small number of clients (I go for the big fish), but others might want to expand exponentially.

1. Innovate to become more accessible. That does not mean lowering your rates! In fact, go ahead and increase your rates by 30 % and create new ways people can access you. That way, you're more accessible, but you're also not sacrificing your earnings. When Meghan did this, she tripled her income within the first quarter. She honed in on her strategy. **Bust the myth that you need to see more people to make more money.**

2. Find innovative work ways: Group coaching programmes. Your client goes through the programme before they have access to the practitioner, building community at the same time. Clients feel amazing before walking into the practitioner's office. Another work way: involve health coaches in your practice. I can't be on the phone to them every day, have other coaches do that. Innovate in delivery of care.

Low down: You provide an evaluation for a client. Instead of spending an hour explaining something you have outlined multiple times before, make a video and send it to the client. Then, provide a 20 minute follow up. That's 20 minutes of your time, but the client gets the same value. **Boom!** And the video can be reused for each new client.

How do you answer when you're coaching people and they think they can't charge as much because they aren't putting in as much time? That question assumes that the **only** value you're giving is your **time**. But the most valuable thing you're giving people is your **strategic thinking and your knowledge**.

You're buying my strategy not my time.

Plus, you're respecting your client's time.

How to put this to your clients: What is the outcome you want to achieve? Explain how you work, lay it all out. If the client is not a good fit, that's fine. Where we can help people with different implementations, we want to do that.

Remember: High-quality care is a person with a **great referral network**. It's a sign of being a person of integrity. You also get referrals that way.

Christine's top tip: I don't take it personally if a client finds me too expensive.

Avoiding Entrepreneurial Burnout (& Identifying it in Your Clients)

> **TOOLBOX**
>
> Free app: Provider Resilience
> Tracks your resilience.

What is burnout?

- Over the top reaction to a scenario that is no different to any other day.
- Not getting enough sleep, chronic fatigue, insomnia, getting sick a lot, weight loss, changes in appetite, aches and pains. Always check medical health first and rule

out anything. Headaches, stomach aches, aching joints, increase drive for junk food, sugar. Anxiety, depression, irritability, anger, pessimism, cynicism, detachment. (These are all yellow flags.) Drop in productivity, forgetfulness, drop in concentration.

- Recency bias: someone asks how you are, and you start telling them how you felt over the last 48 hours only.

If we're seeing many yellow flags or for a longer period, this points to burnout. Anybody can have a bad day. But if it goes on for longer, you need to assess.

What to do.

1. Practise radical self-care: paying attention, having boundaries, setting limits. Knowing when to say yes or no.
2. Pay attention to that in ourselves and clients. Using tech tools to track is so useful (see TOOLBOX).
3. Start an inventory: What am I seeing, how strong are the feelings? The goal is to achieve balance. Am I in balance? Think over your last week / month.

Client example.

There was a client who started to be irritated by little things at work. She found herself being shorter with people and snappier.

She was starting to think, when can I retire? She was waking up and immediately overwhelmed with work. She had anxiety, early signs of depression. She was too tired to do the things she needed to do. She didn't do any exercise and ate unhealthy food.

Intervention: a strategy for her was to start the day off with laughter. With a hit of dopamine. A simple thing like watching funny cat videos first thing. Generally, I don't advise to go on your phone first thing, but for her, watching cat videos for 5 minutes before getting up, was like magic!

It's a simple, low-cost intervention, an example of radical selfcare.

Another example of an intervention for that client: block off time and take breaks. Set aside time for half an hour where she could close the door (open door policy) to take care of important stuff.

IMPORTANT: If you see orange/red flags, you must refer to medical professionals. Flags such as unremitting fatigue, sense of hopelessness, feeling of helplessness, lack of mental flexibility.

Start with breathing: find an app that works for you. Breathe2Relax.

You can control your brain through breathing.

6. Words of Wisdom

Section 6

WORDS OF WISDOM

5 Myths That are Hurting Your Business

1. "All you need to grow an audience is an ads budget." When you're starting out it's better to start organic. Until you have a proven method and are sure about it, know who you're talking to, get testimonials, get results – don't go with ads first. I learnt the hard way where I was selling into a deafening silence. I didn't test it out; I just threw money at it. If anyone tells you that ads will change your life, it's just not true. Try your stuff out, speak in a voice that is authentic to you.

2. "It's just a numbers' game." If you're just concerned with numbers, you forget that you're actually talking

to humans. It's different when you're selling washing powder. Make the distinction between an influencer and a businessperson. Numbers actually don't matter. It's not about quantity, but quality. You don't need a massive following for a successful business. Don't worry about speed either. People stalk stuff they're interested in for a long time.

3. "Content doesn't matter." How are people supposed to find you without content? I don't work nonstop; I'm lazy, so I have a batch system. I work, say, two hours a month on content and everything is batched out over that month. Content is the cheapest way of getting authority, of people finding you. **You want to share your wisdom**. Why are you in business if you don't want people to know what you know? There are so many people out there providing so much value. So, if you're not sharing your wisdom and value, then how are you going to stand out? How are people going to trust you? That's how people get to know you, your personality, your voice. Why people buy from you has more to do with their connection as a person than how good your product is. The advice "don't tell people everything or they won't buy from you" is rubbish! If people need you, they will buy from you. You should be very generous in your blog posts. If people can't afford

me, they can find so much on my blog to help them. https://www.christinemeansbusiness.com/blog/

4. "Online courses are the best business model." This is half rubbish, half true. It's not a good place to start with online courses. **You need to be able to talk to your clients in order to figure out how to do your job.** You can't do that with a course. Only after hearing from people do you know what to put in your course. However, if you've been practicing for a while, a course can be worthwhile. But you will need a lot more people to buy your course than if you go one-on-one. You need a loyal following. If you've never gotten a result for a human, you can't promise that in a course. It takes a lot of energy to market a course.

5. "All coaches are the same, you can do this alone, all marketing strategies and advice work for everyone." **Every business is so different**. People are very different in how they spend money. There are some fundamental truths but so many individual factors. People's health is so personal. From when they find you to investing in you – that's a long period in any business, but especially in health coaching. You can't do it alone. Being in business is the best, but it is tough. Because you provide a service, marketing etc., you have to be in love with yourself, that takes a lot of work. You need a support network for that.

How to Connect with Your Clients (& Guide Them to Success)

The real art of coaching is being able to see when people are ready to change, but they don't know how. Being able to set your own bias aside and see the world through their eyes. What is blocking them? You need to provide a safe space for clients. They're allowed to feel frustration, resistance.

A teacher - student dynamic is not helpful. That kind of dynamic misses out on entire connections. Because the client is afraid to wrong you, to fall off track, to admit when they're struggling. Instead, approach it from the conversational perspective, think "we're a team, we're in this together, we'll figure it out together," like sitting on a couch with a friend.

How can I be there for you?

5 Things I wish I knew as a coach

1. Education matters less than you think it does. You don't need more education to get clients. As a general health coach, for example, you don't need more than your health coach certification to help the average person using your coaching skills and common sense. Of course, go get more degrees if you want to, but don't feel you need to. People

will want to work with you because of your personality. You need to be aware of who you want to serve and what your level of knowledge is. Successes and experience with clients are the most important. I have a good level of education, but I also work with top-level clients (money-wise). Also, my area of expertise means I need to have a more extensive knowledge base. But when you're starting out especially, it's not the most important thing.

2. Vanity metrics don't matter. Small lists or a small Facebook group doesn't matter! Things change so fast. It's all down to algorithms. However, it doesn't hurt to invest in a company who can help you (legitimately) build a small following on whatever platform. Treat your list and social media as if it were thousands, even if you only have fifty. Treat your followers like humans. I purge my list every three months. Also send out emails twice a year to unsubscribe if they're not interested. Send an email: no formatting, just say: "Hi, I'm wondering if you still need my services, Christine." Get rid of those who don't react. They take space in your list, cost you money, skew data, opening leads, etc. I'm not a fan of writing, so I'm not going to expect my email list to convert like crazy.

3. Don't reinvent the wheel. Learn how to repurpose content. (*See Jamie Palmer on repurposing content, Chapter 3.4*). Create high-quality content every week or two. I

just do a Facebook video and my assistant takes care of rest. This increased my organic reach from 56 % to 80 %. You get the same questions over and over so you can talk about the same topics from year to year. You will also learn more, etc. Not every person is following everything you do. Plus, people need repetition for things to stick.

4. Outsourcing. Even if it's just one thing. There will be one thing you're not good at. Like, graphic design. Outsourcing this will free up energy for you. You raise your vibe, your authority, you'll feel like a proper business, it will be a completely different vibe. And if you can say my assistant deals with that, you'll feel like a proper boss. Think about what you need to do, e.g., video. But you don't need to do the transcription. Platforms you can use: Upwork, Fiverr, Facebook groups, agencies, concierge services. Give them a test project and see how it goes. Don't freak out if you invest money, it'll come back to you.

Business grows from the inside out.

Christine's Business Pillars

When I started to build my first businesses Sleep Like A Baby and Sleep Like A Boss, I noticed how much I loved the aspect of creating a business, how good I am at it! I realized I see the gaps in other people's businesses and where they need to fill those black holes to create the best business for them. So that's when I moved into business coaching and Christine Means Business was born.

Over the years, I've done lots of things right and lots of things wrong. With those experiences I've distilled my wisdom into five pillars that every online business should be aware of and check in on regularly. These are especially important for service-based businesses.

Christine's wisdom. Blind spots to avoid.

1. The first big mistake people make is being too vague, too broad about what they do. Most people spend too much time on learning and consuming rather than doing and trying. Just get going. Stop consuming and planning. That's not what is going to get you clients.

2. Don't try to do too much by yourself. You might not want to plan to expand and grow later on – but you should! Otherwise, you end up wearing so many different hats. I **do** think you should try on all those different roles (CEO, tech guy, marketing person, accountant, videographer, etc.) in the beginning, so that you can understand early on where you can outsource as quickly as possible.

3. Don't focus on a look first before figuring out what kind of person you want to work with. If you do that, you'll just have to change everything in three months once you've got experience and start asking the right questions. Caveat: you can always change.

Christine's Pillars with some comments.

1. Branding.

Don't worry about creating the typical client avatar. Don't make a spreadsheet all about JANE: who she is, what she wants, etc. BUT you do need to niche in your content area or area of expertise. The internet is a huge place, so instead of saying I'm a health coach for women, use the three-layered technique: Instead of health, what is it exactly? What area of health? Say, thyroid. Now, dig deeper. What kind of thyroid? Then, instead of saying "women," you can say "Mums, CEOs, age range."

DO NOT WORRY: You're not going to deter anyone.

Your values should be your clients' values. (More important than where they shop, right!?)

My no nos: I don't want to work with people who are impatient and ungrateful.

I love communication, honesty, integrity. I kind of reverse-engineered my niche: I asked myself what are the people like who I don't want to work with? It's easier to know what you don't like in someone else. Don't lower your bar for your clients. They have to reach the bar of your values. My business coach Joanna Hunter has a brilliant trick which is to ask the question: "Are they tall enough?" Just like when riding a rollercoaster. There is a bar. Too short= Tough luck. You do the same with your clients.

You can journal on this but even better is to find someone to talk to – that's what a business coach is for, like me!

2. Pricing and Packaging.

A mistake I see around pricing is that people have set prices that have nothing to do with their level of comfort, they have weird reasons for charging a certain amount: e.g., comparison with other coaches, what they learnt through their training, or what they think they should charge by the hour and then they multiply that. That is almost never sustainable if you want to run a profitable business. My advice: first see what you actually need. Take all your bills from one year, find out how much you need over 12 months and then divide to know what you need monthly. Once you know your monthly rate, then you can start to create your packages. In order to create your packages, you need to know your method. Your method is how you work with people, what you teach, what is the process that you do over and over again. Those are your pillars. They are what makes your method yours. It will always be yours even if someone has exactly the same pillars as you, they will have had different experiences, read different books, had different mentors and coaches. Give it a name that makes sense to you. XYZ method, blueprint, system, etc.

Now, you take your method and divide it into packages. I always say you should be able to sell your method in three different packages: a cheaper, DIY version; a package where you provide the accountability and access, where you tailor everything to your client – that is your traditional one-on-one coaching; and finally, you have your VIP version, which you create by collapsing the time frame, that is, you shortcut the time your client needs to implement something. For example, you teach everything in one day and then offer follow-ups.

Having that objective baseline, knowing how much you need to make each month, allows you to sell with authenticity and alignment.

3. Tech.

Tech can be hugely draining if you don't like it, and it can be a time-waste sinkhole. I do think you have to go through it once so you know how everything works, but I also think if you take too much time over it and it leaves you completely drained, it's the first thing you should outsource. The best thing for you to do if you want to outsource as fast as possible, is to make notes. That way, you create a cooperation manual, SOP (standard operation procedures), so that when you have a new team member you just hand that out and they can take it from there.

Usually, these tasks are not that expensive to outsource.

Your business is like a hotel experience for your clients.

They enter into the lobby, the feel of the place, the scent, the way the receptionist greets you... that is what your tech is for. Your lobby could be your opt-in, your free lead magnet, your greeting is the receptionist, your consistent communication (newsletter, classes, etc.). The onboarding experience when someone becomes your client, if everything goes smoothly, will give you those extra stars.

That is what I do for my clients – I even record tutorials on various tech issues for them. I love going the extra mile. Start by focusing on the final experience or outcome, and then reverse engineer.

Top tip: the first three emails you send once someone has signed up to your mailing list, should be welcoming emails. Don't start selling yet. Welcome them into your hotel, get to know them.

4. Content creation.

    There are two types of content (*I go deeper into this in Chapter 3.3. and 3.4*). Social media is your impulse content, where you connect, it's fresh, short-lived. Long-term content is designed for search-engines, Google, Pinterest, YouTube.

    Content for social media: for me that's Insta, Facebook, Twitter. Those platforms are for your soul clients. You can impart some knowledge on these platforms, people need to know you're good at your job, but it's mainly social, it's mainly what you're about, who you are. This type of content I do spontaneously – more or less. But I do have main topics written down. I write down trigger moments, when I notice that something annoys me, and I investigate that. That takes away the pressure of having to come up with content because I have a steady flow of notes.

    I never want to post because I have to. It just means you're giving off the wrong vibe.

I show up every day to connect with my soul clients.

Long-term content: that is where your blog posts or videos come in. Each one of us has a medium that works best for us, whether it's talking, writing, video. Figure out your fav content first. For me, it's video. Secondly, batch your content. I plan for a whole year, break it down into quarters, months, weeks, and plan content that way. (*See the low down in Chapter 4.1*) Then I redistribute to all the different mediums. So, I take a video, it's edited, I have someone take notes, those notes go into my blog post, the video goes onto YouTube, Anchor (podcast platform) extracts the audio, an intro is added, and it goes out to every podcast platform.

Then, you can also take snippets and create graphics or quotes and you can use the content for your newsletter.

If you don't do outreach and PR, you will be talking to the same people again and again. While it's great to have superfans, you do also need to have new eyeballs on you to make sure you can work with the clients who really need you.

5. Outreach: for me, the best way to do that is collaborations, i.e., webinars, summits, Insta takeovers, courses for a course bundle. Other people entrusting you with their

audience. Another way to outreach is writing. It helps to get media credibility markers. You can either find people who are collaborators or work for different outlets (*Forbes*, *Business Insider*), you can interact with them, give them a quote. Or you can pitch directly.

Pitching: There are different ways to write a story. Personal angle, business point of view, statistics point of view, or you can piggyback on something that's currently trending. I love listicles (3 top tips to...) I also love podcasts: they have very faithful listeners. I find amazing clients on there. Want to get on TV? See Chapter 1.3 for all my tips!

People can get everything online. They hire you for the library in your brain, your access, and your tailoring.

All of this is tough, I'm not going to lie. And it's hard to do it on your own. That is where someone like me comes in. And the best support might come from places you didn't expect, not necessarily from your family and friends but people on the internet. You need an accountability buddy.

I'd love to be yours! Contact me at
https://www.christinemeansbusiness.com/contact/

AFTERWORD

A Word of Warm, Loving Wisdom.

Now you've come to the end of my book, I hope it's been a fantastic ride for you. I hope you are equipped with all the tools you need to run your amazing online business. I want to share some last words of wisdom with you that come from a place of love and warmth.

Be realistic about your time expectations. What I see happening over and over is that people start setting everything up for their business and that takes a lot of energy. After two to three months, you feel like you've done it all. But nothing happens. You're already exhausted because it takes a lot of energy, and you get frustrated. The truth of it is, all you've been doing is giving birth. It's like having a baby. Everything is about getting the business ready; getting a website done, email set up, newsletter down, lead magnet and Insta set up, writing your first blog post, composing your bio. Learning all of these things is like the baby growing in utero. Only then, do you birth your business and, guess what, now you need to help it grow. And then you get frustrated because nobody is opting onto your email list or downloading your lead magnet. You might feel things should start to get going because you've been going for three months, but the truth is, you haven't. You're still really new. It just takes time. (Unless you have an enormous budget to drive ads and even that doesn't guarantee success.)

This is my word of love and a little warning. Just be realistic about time. It also all depends on how much time you put in, the more time you invest, the bigger and quicker the results you'll get. But people tend to underestimate how much work setting up a business is.

Remember to be a **lighthouse**. People need to be aware of you, but you don't budge. People will come to you when they're ready. Grow your audience through collaborations with other lighthouses.

Be realistic and kind to yourself. It's not a race. Everybody gets results in different time frames. Remember that when you feel like quitting. Momentum comes in increments. First, you have really small increments: someone liking your post on Insta, getting a comment. That is worth celebrating. And these small increments will increase and gain momentum. But it takes time. I didn't want to believe that when I was starting out and it took me a few years to become successful even though I did loads.

Finally, remember that starting a business is not the right idea when you're in a dire financial situation and need to make money fast. It will get you into a spiral of financial desperation, you won't make good choices, your vibrations and communication are going to be off, and that is just not how it's supposed to be.

If you're unsure, do it part time. It's totally fine to have a side gig to make sure that the bills get paid.

I'm there for everyone. Reach out to me and see how we can create amazing things together.

GUEST BIO'S

Rebecca Tracey

Rebecca Tracey is the head honcho at The Uncaged Life where she works coaches to get clear on their brand message, create packages that sell, and helps them learn what it actually takes to get and keep clients in this crazy online world (all while working from home with no pants on). Rebecca runs a free online community of over 13k solopreneurs. She started her business while living in a van, and now owns a slightly upgraded van that she uses to go on rock climbing trips for months at a time when she's not running her Uncage Your Business program.

theuncagedlife.com

Jessica Freeman

Jessica Freeman is an Atlanta-based award-winning web designer that helps nutrition and fitness business owners build authority and get more clients. When she's not working with clients, you can find her teaching inside her Better Collective community or on her YouTube channel.

jesscreatives.com

Gina Michnowicz

Gina is a hands-on, fully engaged, client-focused CEO. She built her career intentionally, gaining experience in a variety of disciplines and going deep in marketing and sales within brands, agency, and management consulting. She thinks both strategically and creatively, leading the team to push the envelope with work that both surprises and intrigues audiences in both B2B and B2C markets.

Gina's expertise in brand, digital, and social media has won engagements with clients like Cisco, Disney, 20th Century Fox, Paramount, and Microsoft. For these and other brands, she has led teams from concept to delivery of immersive digital experiences, experiential installations, websites, and bespoke advertising campaigns as the Executive Creative Director.

http://www.thecraftsmanagency.com/

Amanda Daley

Amanda Jane Daley is a leading Business Mentor for Health Coaches worldwide. Renowned for her marketing expertise (with over 19 years of experience!) Amanda has earned recognition by the world's top advertising awards, and has built her own 7-figure coaching business in under 5 years. Founder of the successful health coaching biz 'Fuel Urban Wellness,' Amanda now combines her business + coaching savvy to mentor other health coaches to start their businesses and learn to make $5K+ per month — and has been dubbed the 'leading expert' for Health Coaches who desire a heart-fuelled business and a freedom-based lifestyle.

amandajdaley.com

Stephanie Fiteni

Stephanie is a content marketing strategist and blog coach. She helps Coaches, Consultants, and B2B companies up-level their blogs and websites so they can grow their business with less effort. She turns her clients' traffic-less blogs into lead-generation engines by helping them plan their content, research their keywords, and create content and funnels that will rank and convert. She is a traffic growth specialist and helps clients get leads and book discovery calls in their sleep.

Stephanie coaches clients on a 1:1 basis, sells online courses, and can be booked to design strategies or speak/train live.

stephaniefiteni.com

Travis Baird

Travis Baird is a copywriter for coaches who want to surprise and delight their customers with personality-packed copy. He believes that in order to have an unforgettable brand (and attract more clients), you have to align your story with your ideal customers' desires. Travis co-founded Visualized Copy with his wife, Megan. They're all about understanding your audience at a mind-reader level so that they see themselves in every email and on every page.

https://visualizedcopy.com/

Jamie Palmer

Jamie Palmer is a business strategist and coach for driven entrepreneurs, service providers, and coaches who want to grow and scale their business online with a signature program. She is the creator of the Business Ecosystem Builders program that helps entrepreneurs build their online business simply while creating more freedom, impact, and income.

Jamie's philosophy lays in simplicity and she's introducing Human Design your Business to help entrepreneurs choose the right business model in order to avoid overwhelm that comes with running a business. Knowing who you are as a human being will help you build the business you've always envisioned.

Other programs created by Jamie include Social Made Simple which teaches entrepreneurs how to take the overwhelm out of their social media marketing efforts by turning macro content into micro and nano content, and Productize for Profit, a course that helps service providers map out their offer suite so they never have to write another proposal again.

jamielpalmer.com

Amber McCue

From single mom at the age of 18 to owning two companies that allow her to work from anywhere. Today Amber runs her businesses from Africa, where she currently lives with her family. Amber is the founder of theplanathon.com, threeboudoir. com, empowerandrise.com, and coaches at ambermccue.com. Through her books, speaking, and in her coaching programs, Amber partners with business owners around the world who want to get more done, realize their dreams, and get freedom for themselves.

ambermccue.com

Jillian Smith

Jillian Smith is the Owner & Managing Director of OneTouch Events LLC, headquartered in Atlanta, Georgia, servicing clients in domestic and international destinations. A natural-born organizer of "all things production," Jillian has turned her natural leadership skills and passion into an award-winning event planning firm that focuses on a heightened client and guest experience. Specializing in transformational conferences, workshops & retreats, the team's approach to event planning is simple and streamlined processes with measurable results; your Event ROI.

onetoucheventsllc.com

Kathryn Hofer

Kathryn Hofer is the founder of Modern Planner, an online community designed to take the dread out of planning and help people live more intentionally. Lovingly referred to as the "champion of boundaries and guilt-free intentional living," Kathryn is passionate about helping overwhelmed and overworked people slow down, create space for what matters, and make meaningful progress toward their goals. When she isn't hosting a Planning Party or connecting with the members of her community, you can probably find Kathryn hanging out with her family, spending time outside, or curled up with a good book.

http://modern-planner.com/

Tracy Raftl

Tracy Raftl got her start online in 2011 when she founded the super popular natural acne blog, The Love Vitamin. Now she helps unstoppable women brand themselves online, and builds them impactful, high-converting, personality-driven websites that make them feel confident to go to the next level in their business.

https://tracyraftl.com

Kristin Hartjes

Kristin is a holistic doctor, transformational coach, and business mentor. She helps new coaches overcome feelings of self-doubt, perfectionism, and overwhelm so they can take courageous action in their businesses and their lives. Through practical business strategy and critical inner work, she empowers her clients to create a thriving online business so they can have the freedom they're dreaming of.

kristinhartjes.com

Tara Wagner

Tara Wagner is a lifelong entrepreneur and Breakthrough coach for small business owners. She helps them use a holistic approach to makeover their stressful businesses, so they can work less, increase profits, and stop burning out.

https://xotara.us/

Meghan Walker, ND (inactive)

Meghan Walker, is a naturopathic doctor and Entrepologist (inactive), focusing on the health optimization of female entrepreneurs and game changers. As an entrepreneur, Meghan started and sold her first business while in University and is a Co-founder and past CEO of the digital health media start-up, Bright Almond. She is the host of the Entrepology Podcast, Founder of Entrepology Labs, creator of the women's performance supplement line, Badass Basics and Chief Cheerleader at Clinician Business Labs – a platform to assist clinicians scale and amplify their businesses.

Meghan is fueled by the core belief that when people are well, they can change the world. Meghan views women as natural entrepreneurs, physiologically predestined for creation. She is driven to support them in achieving this potential by optimizing their health and mindset. Meghan has spoken internationally and through multiple media outlets on topics related to women's performance health and entrepreneurship. Most importantly, Meghan is the mother to three little girls, who she is raising alongside her superstar husband in Toronto Ontario.

http://www.meghanwalker.com/

Kendra Perry

Kendra is a former multiple 6-figure Functional Health Coach turned online business strategist for health & wellness practitioners. She is on a mission to stop health coaches from being broke AF by helping them build BOOMING businesses they are in love with. She has currently helped hundreds of health coaches grow their practices, attract consistent clients, and blow up their bank accounts.

She is the creator of the ground-breaking Health Coach Accelerator Method which turns scared, scattered, and self-conscious coaches into confident, focused, and high-performing health entrepreneurs. She is also the founder of the Group Program Academy which teaches coaches to scale their income and impact with online group coaching programs.

Kendra has been featured in Arianna Huffington's Thrive Global, CEO Blog Nation and Authority Magazine for her expertise on sales.

When she isn't getting fired up about business & marketing, you will find her indulging in her love of adrenaline sports in the remote mountains of beautiful British Columbia, Canada.

https://kendraperry.net/